THE WORD&
POWER
CHURCH

THE WORD & POWER CHURCH

What Happens When a Church Experiences All God Has to Offer?

DOUG BANISTER

ZondervanPublishingHouse

Grand Rapids, Michigan

A Division of HarperCollinsPublishers

The Word and Power Church
Copyright © 1999 by Douglas Banister

Requests for information should be addressed to:

📖 ZondervanPublishingHouse
Grand Rapids, Michigan 49530

Library of Congress Cataloging-in-Publication Data

Banister, Doug, 1961–
    The word and power church : what happens when a church experiences all God
has to offer? / Doug Banister.
        p. cm.
    Includes bibliographical references.
    ISBN: 0-310-22710-0 (hc.)
    1. Evangelicalism. 2. Pentecostalism. I. Title.
BR1640.B36 1999
270.8'29—dc21   99-31133
                                                                                  CIP

This edition printed on acid-free paper.

Published in association with the literary agency of Alive Communications, Inc., 1465
Kelly Johnson Blvd. #320, Colorado Springs, CO 80920.

Interior design by Melissa Elenbaas

Printed in the United States of America

99 00 01 02 03 04 05 06 /❖ DC/ 10 9 8 7 6 5 4 3 2 1

For Sandi

CONTENTS

ACKNOWLEDGMENTS

A warm thank you to:

Fellowship Church—for your courage and faith
Mom and Dad—for believing in me
Bryden, Hunter, Sajen, and Ashten—for grace and time
The Haslam and Lawler families—for providing a refuge
    to write and pray
My prayer team—for the gift of intercession
Gary and Debbie Chesney—for a safe place to grow and fail
Jack and Kathy Tarr—for never giving up
Dr. John Jefferson Davis and Dr. Garth Rosell—for presiding
    over the birth of this vision
Jeff Tickson—for making a dream come true
John Sloan—for treating me like Philip Yancey even
    though I'm not
Roberta Truza—for a decade of faithful support
    and friendship
Jon Lawler—for inviting me to Belmont Church
Joe Key—for living the vision
Mike Edwards—for all the ways you have sacrificed through
    the years
Mark Pate—for not going away
Jesus—for your Word and your Spirit

PART ONE
A House Divided Cannot Stand

CHAPTER ONE

MY JOURNEY BEYOND CATEGORIES

I t was a vulnerable time in my life. I was in a distant city, tired and dry from several long years of ministry. My rented red compact idled at a lazy stoplight. I glanced at scribbled directions lying next to my briefcase on the front seat. I had only two blocks to go.

Should I really be doing this? I wondered nervously, thinking for a moment of friends back home who wouldn't approve of where I was about to go. Yet the hunger within me drove me to press on. The light turned green. I made two left turns into the parking lot and stopped in front of my destination.

I had never been in a place like this before. I had heard of them, of course, but usually from distant acquaintances—not the sort of folks I usually hang out with. I felt embarrassed, as an evangelical pastor, to be here. What if someone saw me? Even worse, what if, well . . . what if I was *influenced* by what lurked within?

I walked to the glass doors at the front of the building with the studied casualness of a man who wants to look as if he's done this a hundred times before but really hasn't. My heart pounded as I turned the handle and stepped into the glare of fluorescent lighting shimmering off the jackets of thousands of books. Here I was.

In a charismatic bookstore.

I wandered from row to row, timidly at first, then with more boldness, my eyes drinking in this strange, new, forbidden world. There were books on healing and books on exorcism, books on prophecy and books on speaking in tongues, books on miracles and books on revival, all packaged with bright, foil-embossed covers that hinted dangerously of power and excitement. I slipped a dozen paperbacks from the shelves, drummed my fingers nervously as the clerk put them on my Visa card, and escaped into the night. My foray into the land of the charismatics had come off undetected. At least for now.

What was a nice evangelical boy doing in a place like this? That's an interesting story. And I'd like to tell it to you.

A PROUD LEGACY

I am proud of my evangelical roots. I was saved in a Brethren church, learned how to share the four spiritual laws from a Campus Crusade for Christ staff member, volunteered at a Billy Graham crusade, graduated from two evangelical seminaries, was a pastor in an evangelical denomination, and diligently read *Christianity Today*. I have nothing but profound gratefulness and respect for my mentors in the evangelical world. They have given me a rich legacy. More than anything, they taught me to love the Word of God and to preach it with passion.

The day after I graduated from seminary in 1987, my wife, Sandi, and I packed up our Nissan pickup truck, vowed never again to buy a car without air conditioning, and headed east. God had called us to Knoxville, Tennessee, to plant Fellowship Church. I was twenty-five (almost twenty-six, I reminded everyone).

Money was tight, so I worked part-time jobs tutoring University of Tennessee football players and writing for a magazine that published sermon illustrations. With the time that remained, we planted the church.

THE QUEST FOR PASSION

Those were good days. The focus of our ministry was the Word of God—its authority and its sufficiency. I didn't know much about pastoring, but I did know that God blesses the preaching of his Word. We became a "teaching" church. I spent most of my hours preparing sermons. God did bless. Lives were changed by God's Word. Our tiny core group outgrew a basement, then overflowed a Christian school library, and then filled the cafeteria of a local junior high school with some six hundred worshipers.

Yet something was missing. Our church had become too much like a classroom. We came dangerously close to defining spiritual growth as learning more about the Bible. Our Bible knowledge was increasing, but we had a hard time pressing beyond all the facts about God into the actual presence of God. We were getting to know him *propositionally*, but were not encountering him *personally*.

This was especially true in my own life. My faith had disintegrated into a worldview that worked, a set of principles to live by. I loved the principles. But I had failed to cultivate an intimate relationship with the Person behind the principles. I knew God intellectually, but not experientially. I loved him with my whole mind, but didn't really understand what it meant to love him with my whole heart.

> Our Bible knowledge was increasing, but we had a hard time pressing beyond all the facts about God into the actual presence of God.

All my life I had talked about the importance of "a personal relationship with Jesus." But my relationship wasn't very personal.

I was not living in sin. Our ministry was enjoying a measure of blessing and power. But I lacked a passion for Jesus. During that time I picked up a paperback copy of Jonathan Edwards's classic, *The Religious Affections*. Edwards has managed to write one of the world's dullest books on spiritual passion! It is also one of the most brilliant ones. America's greatest theologian argues with ruthless logic and biblical precision that a true faith is a passionate faith. His words haunted me. His entire book is filled with statements like "who will deny that true religion consists in great measure in vigorous and lively . . . exercises of the heart" and "let it be considered that they who have but little affection have certainly but little religion."[1]

I had to admit that I was a man who had "but little affection" for Jesus, although I had great affection for his Word. I had become a "Bible Deist"—someone who believes that God has revealed his will for us in the Bible, but that he is not personally involved in how we live those principles out.

THE ARGUMENTS DIDN'T HOLD UP

The summer of 1992 found Fellowship's young congregation methodically walking through Paul's first letter to the church of Corinth. Chapter 12, Paul's famous passage on the so-called charismatic gifts,[2] hung like an August thunderhead on the horizon of our study. I wondered if we might all get wet. Here's the controversial part:

> Now to each one the manifestation of the Spirit is given for the common good. To one there is given through the Spirit the message of wisdom, to another the message of knowledge by means of the same Spirit, to another faith by the same Spirit, to another gifts of healing by that one Spirit, to another miraculous powers, to another prophecy, to another distinguishing between spirits, to another speaking in different kinds of tongues, and to still another the interpretation of tongues. All these are the work of the one and the same Spirit, and he gives them to each one, just as he determines.

There were only sunny skies ahead when we began our study of 1 Corinthians the year before. I was prepared to teach what I was taught in seminary: *There are no miraculous gifts of the Holy Spirit today. Gifts like prophecy, tongues, and healing were limited to the first century and were used primarily by the apostles to authenticate their church-planting ministry in a time when the New Testament was not yet complete.* This is called the doctrine of cessation.

Over lunch in the spring of 1992, a friend gave me a tattered copy of a little paperback called *They Speak With Other Tongues.* The author, *Guideposts* editor John Sherrill, set out to write a book refuting the charismatic movement. Sherrill's skepticism was replaced with spiritual hunger as he pressed further into what God was up to in the charismatic renewal of the sixties. Sherrill ended the book a charismatic!

Sherrill's story jarred me. It was the first time I had read anything describing the charismatic movement positively. What troubled me even more was a brief section in which Sherrill discusses the primary arguments for the doctrine of cessation and then refutes each one. His arguments made sense!

I decided it was time to use the study skills I had learned in seminary to find out for myself what the biblical text really meant. I wrote down each of the seven major arguments for cessation. Then I began examining each argument by asking one question: Does the Bible really teach this? I will never forget sitting at my desk in a mountain cabin, surrounded by commentaries and reference tools, watching each argument crumble before my eyes. I was terrified of what lay before me—an interpretation that differed from what I had always been taught.[3]

My seminary professors had taught me the important Bible study method known as the "checking" principle. This principle simply says that when you have done your own study of the text, always check what you have found with what good scholars have said. Panicking, I began to turn to some of my evangelical mentors. Surely they would show me my errors and return me to the narrow way.

They did not. One trusted scholar after another affirmed what I now feared to be true: the Bible simply does not teach that the charismatic gifts have ceased.

My first surprise came when I read what the great evangelical British preacher D. Martyn Lloyd-Jones had to say on the subject. Lloyd-Jones never preached anything halfway, and this was no exception. He taught that it was foolish to believe that the gifts had ceased. Later, I listened to a tape by John Piper, a respected evangelical leader, pastor, and author. He gently went through the arguments and said that as much as he respected those who believed the gifts had ceased, he could not make that argument biblically. J. I. Packer's writings on

> I was terrified of what lay before me — an interpretation that differed from what I had always been taught

the subject also assumed that these gifts could be available today. The final blow to cessation for me personally came when I read D. A. Carson's commentary on 1 Corinthians 12–14. Dr. Carson is a leading evangelical New Testament scholar and a professor at Trinity Evangelical Divinity School, my denomination's seminary. He, too, concluded that nowhere does the Bible teach that God cannot give these gifts to the church today.

I was trapped! My evangelical training compelled me to let the text lead me. Yet the text was leading me into beliefs that many evangelicals in those days didn't agree with. Reluctantly I took my newfound convictions to the elder board of the church. Together we considered each argument, discussing and at times arguing over each point late into the night. Those were long and painful meetings. One elder eventually left our church over these issues. He is a dear brother, and his departure left a gaping hole. Yet, when the dust had settled, we had rejected the doctrine of cessation because we didn't see it taught in Scripture.

Not much changed in our church besides our doctrinal statement after I preached through 1 Corinthians 12–14 in the summer of 1992. Suddenly, however, the apostle Paul had another matter he could speak to us about. In a sense, we had a "lost chapter" to reexamine, a chapter we had thought didn't have anything to say to the church today. This "new" portion of Scripture challenged my Bible deism. Suddenly I was thrust into the presence of a talking God, a healing God, a God of the Now and the Then. Little did I know that I would soon meet this God in a way I had never imagined.

AN ENCOUNTER IN A CABIN

My friend John and I had often talked about this "new passage," wondering what it looked like in practice. John had attended a church of a mainline denomination in Nashville that was learning about these gifts. The pastor was his good friend and invited us to spend an evening with him. A few weeks later we were in Pastor Don's office. Don had a Ph.D. in New Testament and taught Greek at a local seminary. He also memorized entire books of Scripture. He was a Word man, and I connected with him. Yet something was different about Don and the people in his church. The Spirit seemed tangibly present. I felt like crying later that night during the worship service, and I didn't know why.

The next day I was in a cabin fasting and praying, still shaken by what we had experienced the night before. I could tell that we had been in the presence of God, and I wanted more. I fell on my face and cried out, "Lord, all I know is, I want more of you. I'm dry. I'm hungry. I'm tired of knowing you from a distance. I want to know you intimately, personally. I don't just want to know about you, I want to know *you*."

A torrent of words in a language I had never spoken before welled up within me and poured out through my lips. I didn't know what I was saying, but sensed my soul worshiping God with a passion I had never experienced before. I felt deep remorse for the sins in my life as I pressed closer to the heart of God. Time seemed to stop, but I believe this went on for two hours. I had received the gift of spiritual language. I was praying in tongues.

(I have been sitting at my computer for some time now, wondering if I should hit the delete key and wipe out what I just shared with you. I am afraid that some of my evangelical readers might close the book, fearing yet another "charismatic conversion" novel like the ones that were so popular in the sixties. I promise you, that's not where we are headed. I decided to share this story with you not because of my experience, but because of where God led me through that experience. Hang on, dear reader, and try to finish the chapter.)

The encounter in the cabin reminded me of a muggy summer evening years before when Sandi and I shared our first kiss. We had been in love for some time. The first kiss drew us into a deeper intimacy. Now these two hours in the cabin this day were like a "first kiss" with God.

The grass really did look greener on the other side of the fence in those early months. *Maybe the charismatics do have the answers,* I thought. I read several more books (hence the visit to the charismatic bookstore), attended a number of charismatic worship services, and listened to tapes from charismatic conference speakers. I also swung out of balance. I bruised my wife's feelings by encouraging ✓ her to seek this gift even when she wasn't really interested in praying in tongues. She felt that I was calling her spirituality "second class." Looking back, I think she was right.

Grass is just grass. And it wasn't really greener on the charismatic side of the fence. I loved the worship, the emphasis on prayer, the expectant hope for God to do something big now, the eagerness to hear God speak. Yet I often left mentally empty. The preaching was sincere and earnest, but often shallow and not carefully rooted in the text. I enjoyed the emphasis on divine healing, but noted little understanding of the role of suffering in making us holy. I loved the sense of immediacy ("You can be set free—tonight!"), but failed to hear a corresponding emphasis on the progressive role of sanctification. I was excited to be with people who believed that all of God's gifts were for today, but was disappointed that only the miraculous gifts seemed to matter. I heard a lot about tongues and prophecy and healing, but heard little about service, helps, and administration.

CAN WE HAVE THE BEST OF BOTH WORLDS?

I now had a foot in both camps. As an evangelical, I loved the Word but longed for more of the Spirit. As someone who had begun to drink from the water of the charismatic renewal, I loved the emphasis on the Spirit's power, but saw that this power needed to be wedded with a stronger rooting in the Word. I saw strengths and weaknesses in both traditions. Both camps hold a piece of the puzzle the other needs.

Yet the two camps have been totally isolated from each other. We have different publishers, different authors, different seminaries, different magazines, and different conferences.

There is more than ignorance dividing charismatics and evangelicals. There is hostility. I left seminary with a deep disdain for charismatics. Charismatics have often resented their evangelical brothers and sisters as well. A family feud has been running between the two sides for a generation now. Some of my deepest wounds in ministry have come over this issue. I have wept as dear friends, convinced that it was impossible for charismatics and evangelicals to live together in the same family, have left our church. I remember one long afternoon when my three o'clock appointment came in to tell me he was leaving because we had become too charismatic. My four o'clock appointee came in to tell me she was leaving because we had not become charismatic enough.

It has been painful, but we have pressed on, trying to find the middle way. Today, appointments like the ones I had that sad afternoon are rare. Instead, I am watching God raise up a new generation of Christians who aren't interested in fighting yesterday's battles. They are hungry for the Word and thirsty for the Spirit. They are tired of "either–or." They want both. Some three thousand people worship with us now. I am beginning to understand how much people long for a balanced church that offers the best of both the charismatic and the evangelical worlds. Over and over again I hear people at Fellowship say, "Finally, a church that is balanced!" "Finally, a church where I can get grounded in the Word and touched in my heart!" "Finally, a church that is alive to the Spirit and grounded in the Word!"

> I am watching God raise up a new generation of Christians who aren't interested in fighting yesterday's battles.

What's happening at Fellowship is happening in churches across America. The walls that have divided charismatics and evangelicals are crumbling. Evangelicals are thirsting for more of God's Spirit. Charismatics are hungering for more of God's Word. Charismatics and evangelicals are learning from each other. Resentment is being replaced with respect. God is rewriting the categories that have divided us for nearly a hundred years. One evangelical leader I know observes, "Our children won't even know there was a difference between charismatics and evangelicals. It will become a dead issue." Many believers on both sides agree.

Think of the charismatic and evangelical traditions as two mighty spiritual rivers flowing through our century. Today the two rivers are merging into one mighty flood of spiritual power. God is blending the strengths of both the evangelical and charismatic traditions together in churches across America. I call these *word and power churches.*

I am writing these words on the plane home from Germany, where I was speaking at a conference for my denomination's missionaries. Europe is now entirely post-Christian, dotted with towering but empty churches that are relics of a long-dead faith. America is spiritually only a generation behind Europe. We, too, are increasingly becoming a secular nation. Church attendance is dropping: sixty churches close their doors every week. Rapidly becoming marginalized by the popular culture, the church is increasingly seen as vague and irrelevant to the real issues of life. True, many megachurches are growing; but if you probe deeper, you'll find their ranks filled up not with new converts, but with refugees from dying churches. There is not one county in America that has a higher percentage of Christians living in it today than were there ten years ago. Not one!

George Barna tells us that the baby boomers gave church a chance, but have snuck out the back door. Even more ominous are the data now coming in on the busters, twenty-somethings who represent the future church of America. When busters have needs, the church isn't even on the short list of places they would turn to for help. One pastor in Boston interviewed a large number of busters and asked them what they were looking for in a church. Their answer surprised him: "Why would we look for a church in the first place?"

These are not days to be complacent. Our nation is at a critical juncture and is poised to reject the Christian faith forever. Dare we go about business as usual? Dare we ignore what Christians have to offer one another? Could it be that God raised up *both* evangelical and charismatic traditions in our time because a healthy, vibrant church needs what both have learned about spiritual life and ministry? Could it be that God raised up *both* evangelical and charismatic traditions because he knew that the post-Christian mission field we are called to conquer craves a God of Truth *and* Power?

Both the evangelical and the charismatic traditions bring a rich legacy to the church.

The evangelical legacy includes

Expository preaching
An emphasis on the authority and sufficiency of Scripture
A realistic affirmation that the kingdom of God is not fully here
A belief that spiritual growth is a process
A belief that the Word must be studied in community

The charismatic legacy includes

An emphasis on prayer
A hopeful affirmation that the kingdom is here in part
A belief that God speaks today
An emphasis on participatory worship
A belief that the Spirit must be experienced in community

Word and power churches seek to bring together the best of both charismatic and evangelical worlds. Too dangerous? Too risky? Maybe so, but the risk we face in creating word and power churches pales in comparison with the risk of losing our culture.

CONFIRMATION FROM AN UNLIKELY PLACE

Jim Collins is a former Stanford Business School professor who spent six years researching great companies that had a track record of success over several generations. He grouped the great companies into gold medal and bronze medal categories. Bronze medal companies performed well over time. Gold medal companies performed extremely well over the same period. Collins wanted to find out what made the difference. His findings are written up in his best-selling book *Built to Last*.

> Dare we go about business as usual? Dare we ignore what Christians have to offer one another?

Collins observed that companies—like people—have a tendency to think in terms of "either–or" instead of "both–and." Most companies, he says, believe their options force them to choose between competing opportunities. For example, a company can choose *either* to make a profit *or* to serve the needs of humanity. Collins then shows that highly visionary companies have the ability to embrace both extremes of a number of dimensions at the same time. Instead of being oppressed by the "tyranny of the OR," these companies liberate themselves with the "genius of the AND"; instead of choosing between A *or* B, they figure out a way to have both A *and* B. He cites as an example a pharmaceutical company that figured out how to *both* make a profit *and* serve the needs of humanity *at the same time.* This ability to resist the natural tendency to split the world into competing options, Collins argues, is one secret to a great organization's success.[4]

Irrational? Perhaps. Rare? Yes. Difficult? Absolutely! But as F. Scott Fitzgerald pointed out, "The test of first-rate intelligence is the ability to hold to opposed ideas in the mind at the same time, and still retain the ability to function."[5]

It's not hard to see how the church is enslaved by the tyranny of an "either–or" approach. One way to view the history of Christianity is to see the body of Christ swinging from one extreme to the other, rarely finding the middle way. Our tendency to swing is still present today. We must be either liturgical or contemporary, either liberal or fundamental, either dispensational or Reformed, either socially active or evangelistic. And we must be either charismatic or evangelical.

Let's apply the "genius of the AND" to the one organization that truly is *built to last*, the church. Let's build word and power churches, churches that bring together the best of the evangelical and charismatic traditions.

It can be done. I am the pastor of a word and power church. Our seats are filled each Sunday with evangelicals thirsty for the Spirit and charismatics hungry for the Word. I believe our growth has much to do with our willingness to go beyond tolerating one another as evangelicals or charismatics to actually learning from one another. We are a church that is trying to embrace the principles from both traditions. It has not been easy, and we have a long way to go. But I am convinced we are on the right track. I am also convinced a lot of Christians want to go in this direction with us.

Are you one?

I am writing this book for anyone who is tired of fighting yesterday's battles, who is eager to move beyond categories and to build churches empowered by *both* Word and Spirit. I am writing this book for anyone who sees God powerfully at work in *both* the charismatic and the evangelical movements. I am writing this book for charismatics who want more of the Word *and* evangelicals who want more of the Spirit. I am writing this book for anyone who wants to serve God in spirit *and* in truth. I am writing this book for all who want to love Jesus with all their minds *and* all their souls. I am writing this book for our neighbors who know nothing about theological terms but are longing for a God they can both know and experience. And I am writing this book for good people in good churches who don't want to give up who they are but want to become all they can be.

But are the walls really crumbling? Is God really up to something new? The next chapter shows that the answer is an unqualified "Yes!"

STUDY QUESTIONS

1. Describe your spiritual roots. What events or people have shaped the way you experience God? Discuss what you especially value in the rich legacy of your tradition.

2. Discuss the legacy of the other tradition. What do you especially appreciate in it?

3. Discuss the statement that "a healthy, vibrant church needs what both [traditions] have learned about spiritual life and ministry." Is your church being prepared to step toward the goal of embracing both traditions? How can you address the issues that would prevent this growth?

TRUCE: IT'S TIME TO STOP FIGHTING YESTERDAY'S WAR

On March 9, 1974, Lieutenant Hiroo Onoda of the Japanese army walked out of the Philippine jungle and surrendered, ending a thirty-year ordeal. No one had informed the lieutenant that World War II had ended. His biographer explains, "Year after year he continued with his efforts to evade capture and stay alive, convinced that World War II was still being fought, and waiting for the day when his fellow soldiers would return victorious."[1]

The soldier recalls what he was thinking the moment he finally found out the war was over: "We really lost the war! . . . Suddenly everything went black. A storm raged inside of me. I felt like a fool. . . . Worse than that, what had I been doing for all these years?"[2]

That's a good question to ask yourself when you have been fighting a war that was over a generation ago. It is a question many church members ought to ask as well as we consider the charismatic-evangelical war that has been raging far too long: What have we been doing for all these years? Why are we still fighting a war that has long since been over?

There is no denying it: our century *has* witnessed a bloody battle between charismatics and evangelicals. The feud between our fundamentalist and Pentecostal grandparents began around the turn of the century. We won't appreciate how far we have come without first admitting where we have been.

BLOODY BATTLES

A few hours after midnight on the first day of the second year of the twentieth century, a Bible student named Agnes Ozman asked her teacher, Charles Parham, to lay hands on her and pray for her to be baptized with the Holy Ghost. He did, she was, and Pentecostalism was born. Several years later, the famous Azusa Street revival exploded in an old abandoned church building in Los Angeles. The revival was marked by many strange phenomena, such as speaking in tongues and "falling under the power" of the Spirit. The revival continued for three years, spawning one of the most significant spiritual movements in recent church history: Pentecostalism. Today the three biggest churches in the world are Pentecostal, and Pentecostal/charismatic churches are growing around the world at a rate of fifty-four thousand members a day.[3]

Pentecostalism was not well received by the fundamentalists. One leader called the leaders of the Azusa Street revival "rulers of spiritual Sodom," described speaking in tongues as "this satanic gibberish," and called Pentecostal worship services "the climax of demon worship." Another called the movement "the last vomit of Satan."

Sometimes the fighting went beyond words. Preachers reported instances of being beaten, gagged, shot, thrown in jail, or threatened with death and mutilation. Others reported having churches burned and tents toppled. One Church of God preacher in Mississippi claimed that in 1917 "two men covered him with revolvers, gagged him, and dragged him ... through the woods where they beat him black and blue with a buggy trace, struck him a blow over the eye with a revolver, and broke two of his ribs by kicking him in the side."[4]

Not surprisingly, Pentecostalism kept a safe distance from the rest of the body of Christ for the first half of this century. However, on Sunday, April 3, 1960, Episcopal priest Dennis Bennett told his congregation of his new experience of receiving the baptism of the Holy Spirit and speaking in tongues. The reaction of his congregation foreshadowed the turmoil of what was to come: A man stood on a chair and yelled, "Throw out the d_____ tongues speakers." Bennett soon lost his job. *Time* and *Newsweek* picked up the story, and a surge of interest in the charismatic gifts swept the mainline denominations. The charismatic renewal was born.

The sixties and seventies were times of violent division as local churches, seminaries, and whole denominations grappled with these "new" gifts and their place in the body. Once again, bitter rhetoric spewed forth from both sides, reminiscent of the first days of the

Azusa revival. Once again, those practicing the charismatic gifts were dismissed as satanic. Evangelicals toughened up their doctrinal statements, ensuring that tongues speakers would not be called as pastors or teachers in their schools.

Civil war requires two armies. Charismatics and Pentecostals have also committed war crimes. Every evangelical pastor knows a horror story about how an overzealous charismatic brother split a church. I have handed Kleenex to more than one sister who quietly shared the humiliation she felt when her friends tried to pressure her to speak in tongues, explaining that she couldn't be sure she was really saved if she did not. Evangelicals have often felt judged by charismatics and Pentecostals. I am reminded of the sign in front of the Pentecostal church in our town that read, "No tongues, no salvation," thus sentencing well over half of the body of Christ to an eternity in a tongueless hell.

Yes, there have been wars.

But God has declared a truce. Charismatics and evangelicals are working together today in unprecedented ways. One leader recently told me that he believed ten years from now the terms *evangelical* and *charismatic* would no longer be in use. Dr. Gordon Fee of Regent Seminary is a Pentecostal scholar whose work is widely respected by evangelical scholars. I asked him whether he thought the war between charismatics and evangelicals that was so bloody a generation ago was still going on in academic circles. "The war is over," he said flatly. "The only people who are still arguing about it are talking among themselves."

> God has declared a truce. Charismatics and evangelicals are working together today in unprecedented ways.

TWO RIVERS

I slip away each Thursday to fast and pray. Friends provide a cabin on the grounds of a peaceful, secluded retreat center called Two Rivers. The retreat gets its name because it overlooks the spot where the Little River and the Tennessee River converge. One Thursday afternoon I was gazing over the river bend where the powerful, deep waters of the two rivers merge into one.

That's what God is doing today, I thought. *The two rivers are becoming one.* The charismatic movement and the evangelical movement are like two mighty rivers surging through the twentieth century. The first river represents the word churches. The word churches have championed the inerrancy of Scripture and obedience to its authority in every realm of life. These churches have defended the truth whenever and wherever it has been attacked. Word churches include the fundamentalist, dispensationalist, and Reformed churches. Word churches are often referred to as evangelical churches.

The second river represents the power churches. The power churches have championed the Person and power of the Holy Spirit in the church's life and witness. The power churches have called the church to experience God, to seek his power, to expect the supernatural and the transformation of life by the Spirit. Power churches include Pentecostal and charismatic churches.

These two great rivers have flowed side by side for a century. Now the two rivers are becoming one mighty torrent of spiritual power. God is bringing together the best of the charismatic and evangelical worlds to create word and power churches, churches anchored in the Word and alive in the Spirit. We have always been a people of the Book and the Wind, the law and the Spirit, the *logos* and the *ruach*.

For several years now, I have been stuffing a file with assorted magazine clippings, quotes, Internet stories, e-mail messages, and newspaper articles that chronicle the amazing merger that is taking place. What follows is a sampling of different ways God is bringing evangelicals and charismatics together.

∽

It is Valentine's Day 1996. Thirty-six thousand pastors from every denomination cram the Atlanta Dome for the first-ever Promise Keepers Clergy Conference. The platform team includes the presidents of Dallas Seminary and Moody Bible Institute, a Pentecostal pastor, and, of course, Promise Keepers founder Bill McCartney, who is a member of a Vineyard church. The conference emcee is an African-American charismatic who skillfully blends traditional and contemporary hymns and choruses in a way that everyone seems comfortable with. Some stand up and raise their hands, some worship quietly in their seats. Christian singer Steve Green electrifies the audience with his song about Christian unity, "Let the Walls Fall Down."

ᴌᴏ

Christianity Today is the voice of evangelicalism. Founded by Billy Graham and originally edited by the great evangelical scholar Carl F. H. Henry, the magazine was created in 1956 to cast the evangelical vision. It is significant, then, that in June 1996 the magazine's cover story discussed a book on the Holy Spirit by Pentecostal scholar Gordon Fee. The article affirms Fee's work and encourages evangelical readers to learn from him.

ᴌᴏ

Several leading evangelical seminaries have already embraced the wonderful diversity of both evangelical and charismatic traditions. Gordon-Conwell Theological Seminary, a leading evangelical institution, had a Pentecostal president, Dr. Robert E. Cooley, for thirteen years. Students from the Assemblies of God nearly outnumber Presbyterians and Baptists at Gordon-Conwell. The president of Fuller Seminary, another leading evangelical school, is Dr. Richard Mouw, an evangelical; the seminary's provost is Dr. Russell Spittler, a Pentecostal. I asked Dr. Spittler to comment about my observation that the two rivers are becoming one. "We experience exactly that here at Fuller," he said. "Presbyterians form the largest student body, then the Baptists, then the charismatics and Pentecostals." Regent Seminary in Vancouver, British Columbia, is another example. Faculty and students range from Anglican to Pentecostal. Professor Fee reports that "there is no sense of tension at all here. The lines have been totally redrawn."

ᴌᴏ

Jack Hayford, a leading Pentecostal pastor, published *The Beauty of Spiritual Language*. In this book Hayford takes the dramatic step of breaking ranks with his tradition and argues that speaking in tongues is not the only evidence of being Spirit-filled, thus toppling a major barrier between the two traditions. The book, which still strongly encourages praying in a spiritual language, sells well among evangelicals and charismatics alike.

ᴌᴏ

My wife is a member of the sacred dance ministry in our church. Sacred dance is one of many art forms that God is bringing back into the church today. Each June she attends a sacred dance conference at a large Baptist church. (Baptists and dancing? God is doing something new!) The conference participants are a mix of charismatics and evangelicals who share a love for the arts and especially for dance. I asked Sandi if there was any tension between the two groups. She replied that it simply wasn't an issue.

&

The exploding prayer movement is led by both evangelicals and charismatics. For example, the nationally televised Concerts of Prayer held each year in May is led by a who's who of evangelical and charismatic leaders. Bill Bright prays beside Jack Hayford. The president of Moody Bible Institute is on the platform with the president of the Assemblies of God.

In October 1995, forty-four million Christians united to pray for the breakthrough of the gospel into one hundred world-class cities. The effort, called "Praying Through the Window II," was the largest prayer effort in the history of the Christian church. Luis Bush, a Presbyterian from Argentina, led the effort. Charismatic and Pentecostal organizations like the Christian Broadcasting Network, Youth With a Mission, Oral Roberts University, and *Charisma* magazine joined with many others to gather together intercessors from around the world. Charismatic pastor Ted Haggard, another leader of the movement, told me,

> By now, most evangelicals and charismatics have concluded that one group cannot accomplish the goal of reaching the lost without the strength of the other. Thinking evangelicals no longer see themselves as biblically superior to charismatics, and charismatics no longer see themselves as more spiritual than evangelicals.

We are finding that to be true here in Knoxville. We hosted our first Prayer Summit for pastors in March. Sixty pastors from a wide range of denominations met for four days of prayer for the city. "By the last day," one pastor reports, "we were just the body of Christ. It didn't matter what tradition we were from."

Deep brokenness marked the meetings. "I've not spoken well of you or of your church," an evangelical pastor confessed to an Assemblies of God pastor. "Will you forgive me?" "I've had spiritual pride toward the rest of the body . . . thought I was better than you guys because of the gifts," a Pentecostal pastor shared. "I'm so sorry. Will you forgive me?"

Prayer cells birthed at the summit now meet all over the city. My prayer cell includes Baptists, charismatics, and Presbyterians. Our prayer times are among the richest I have ever experienced. My favorite line: "You know," an evangelical pastor confesses, "I'm realizing that there really is something to spiritual warfare." "Careful, brother," says his charismatic prayer partner. "Let's keep our focus on Jesus, not on demons."

∽

God is also drawing evangelicals and charismatics together on the mission field. "In many parts of the world," says Joe Wasmond, International Director of Freedom in Christ Ministries, "unity between evangelicals and charismatics 'is almost a given.'" This is especially the case in corners of the world ravaged by war and famine. Wasmond, who travels the world each year as a conference speaker, says, "When you are scrounging for food or dodging bullets, it doesn't make any difference what theological flavor your brother is. You stick together because you need each other." Even prosperous nations are watching both traditions unite against a creeping secularism. Some examples:

> God is also drawing evangelicals and charismatics together on the mission field.

- The evangelical Christian and Missionary Alliance churches call a nationwide spiritual warfare conference for the nation of Ecuador. They invite platform speakers from both evangelical and Pentecostal churches. The speakers come, bringing their people with them. Church leaders report that this is the first time in their nation's history that people from both groups have cooperated in a nationwide event.
- Ten thousand would-be worshipers are turned away from a prayer meeting in Cali, Colombia, because the soccer stadium only holds sixty thousand. Those who do make it through the turnstiles pray through the night for their city, notorious in the past as the headquarters of the infamous Columbia drug cartel. The massive crowd is a mix of evangelical and charismatic believers.

- A prayer team from Fellowship Church ministers in Vietnam. On the last evening of our trip we dine with a pastor from one of Vietnam's charismatic house churches. "The body of Christ has been divided over the gifts for many years," he tells us. Today the leaders of the evangelical and charismatic church movements are beginning to work together again as they confront the overwhelming task of evangelizing Vietnam.
- A missionary couple from Eastern Europe describes how the two rivers are merging in their city. There are two extremes in their community—a radical Pentecostal group mired in mysticism and a radical fundamentalist group mired in legalism. His vision, the missionary tells me, is to provide a middle road between these two extremes, a church of both word and power.

Mission watchers are noting that this is a worldwide trend. One writer comments:

> Christian unity is helping world evangelization. . . . Waves of repentance and reconciliation among races, denominations and ministries have paved the ways for unprecedented joint efforts. Strategic alliances, even between groups historically suspicious of one another, are making possible the wise use of both funds and personnel in missions. A strong threefold chord of traditional evangelicals, charismatics and members of mainline denominations has been woven by the Holy Spirit. Massive cooperation efforts among ministries great and small could produce a harvest of at least 1 billion souls in the next five years.[5]

↜

A quick surf of the Internet uncovers even more evidence that the two rivers are indeed merging. When I asked my secretary to browse the Net, she came up with articles about Reformed Charismatics and Charismatic Methodists! Talk about oxymorons!

The article about the former begins, "Reformed Charismatics (RCs) is a designation that describes Christians who have emerged mainly from the charismatic movement . . . who are searching for a greater theological substance than what they encountered in the emotionally laden, often doctrinally deficient charismatic movement."[6] Notice that the author consciously chooses to recognize both traditions in his title. He is proud of both his evangelical and his charismatic roots.

The Methodist writer laments over the spiritual decline of his denomination. He wonders whether God has left his beloved church and reluctantly asks if the future belongs to the Pentecostals. "I am not willing to concede this," he says, and then pleads for a merger of the charismatic renewal with the original evangelical roots of Methodism. He offers a cry for a word and power church. "As Wesleyan Christians," he writes, "we need to reclaim our heritage *of experiential religion with biblical authority.*"[7]

~~

Willow Creek Community Church, with its sixteen thousand members, is famous for its contemporary evangelicalism. Each August, five thousand leaders from around the world cram the Willow Creek campus in Barrington, Illinois, for an annual Leadership Summit.

> Jesus teaches us to look around and ask, "What is the Father doing?" You don't have to look very far to see.

The August 1998 conference featured well-known evangelical speakers like Joe Stowell of Moody Bible Institute. The conference *worship* was led by Darlene Zschech, worship leader of the charismatic Hills Christian Life Center in Castle Hill, Australia. Zschech ("a Willow favorite," according to the brochure) has become popular in the States with her Hillsongs worship CDs, which are high-energy praise songs similar to the kind you would find at the Pensacola Revival in Florida.

LESSONS FROM DUNKIRK

Jesus teaches us to look around and ask, "What is the Father doing?" (John 5:17–20). You don't have to look very far to see. Lines are being redrawn, categories are collapsing, old paradigms are giving way to new ones. The cartoon character Pogo was wrong when he said, "We have met the enemy, and they are us." We are not the enemy. We can't afford any more casualties to friendly fire while the real Enemy continues his stealth campaign against the kingdom of God.

The spring of 1940 found Hitler's panzer divisions mopping up the French troops and preparing for a siege of Great Britain. The

Dutch had already surrendered, as had the Belgians. The British army foundered on the coast of France in the channel port of Dunkirk.

Nearly a quarter-million young British soldiers and over a hundred thousand Allied troops were preparing to die. The Fuehrer's troops, only a few miles away in the hills of France, closed in on an easy kill. The Royal Navy had enough ships to save barely seventeen thousand men, and the House of Commons was told to brace itself for "hard and heavy tidings." Then, while a despairing world watched with fading hope, a bizarre fleet of ships appeared on the horizon of the English Channel. Trawlers, tugs, fishing sloops, lifeboats, sailboats, pleasure crafts, an island ferry named *Gracie Fields*, and even the America's Cup challenger *Endeavor*, all manned by civilian sailors, sped to the rescue. The ragtag armada eventually rescued 338,682 men and returned them home to the shores of England, as pilots of the Royal Air Force jockeyed with the German Luftwaffe in the skies above the channel. It was one of the most remarkable naval operations in history.[8]

Today Dunkirk is synonymous with courage and bravery, a hallowed memory of a nation at her finest hour. May the days we now live in be the church's Dunkirk, our finest hour, as we lay aside the petty differences that are the luxury of peacetime and join forces against our common foe.

STUDY QUESTIONS

1. Have you experienced hostility between the two traditions? How has that affected you or others around you?

2. Of the many stories that illustrate how the two traditions are blending together, which one most touched you? Have you seen other instances of reconciliation between the two traditions?

3. Is it helpful to compare the church's ministry to warfare? Who is your church battling, the true Enemy or other Christians? How can your church support or be supported by other Christian traditions?

Chapter Three

THE QUEST FOR SOMETHING MORE

I was once asked to speak on the subject "How to Grow a Church in the Nineties." I considered titling the talk, "Beats Me!" You've read enough by now to know that the secret to our growth is not my great communication skills. Max Lucado I am not. I am a decent preacher, but I have a high-pitched voice that would probably annoy you if you heard me on tape. There are many better preachers out there than the one Fellowship hears every week. The reason is not my great leadership skills, either. This church outgrew my capacity to lead it about eleven years ago. I look at pastors like Bill Hybels of Willow Creek or Jack Hayford of the Church on the Way in Van Nuys, California, and say, "Now that is what a megachurch pastor looks like!" These men are strong, bold, visionary leaders who are spiritually sensitive but have the leadership skills to match any corporate CEO. I don't.

This may all sound like false humility to you, but it's a matter of deep anguish for me and at times has almost driven me out of the ministry. I am well aware of the "founders syndrome," that bothersome organizational law that says that usually the people who start organizations can't keep them growing into the future. More than once I have asked the Lord, "Is my run done here? This is too big for me, Father. Shouldn't we get somebody in here who knows what he is doing?" During the spring of 1997 God led me through a season of deep pain and discouragement as I wrestled with these questions. The answers he gave me, and the way he gave them, are a major reason why I am writing this book.

Our church building campaign had not gone well, and I felt responsible. I had just finished a series of sermons on the gift of spiritual language, calling our body to honor one another regardless of what gifts we enjoyed. The series went well but depleted my spiritual reserves. My evenings were spent trying frantically to complete my doctoral dissertation. Lurking behind all this was my eight-year-old daughter Bryden's battle with cancer. She had completed her chemotherapy, but beneath the surface Sandi and I were wrestling with how long she would be in remission. I found myself spinning into depression and hating myself for it: senior pastors aren't supposed to have these kinds of problems!

Bill Hybels and John Maxwell, two of evangelicalism's most notable leaders, came to our city during this time to teach a conference on church leadership. Most of my staff went, but I did not. I am embarrassed to admit it, but at the time, I felt intimidated by these two giants of the faith and was reminded by their presence of who I wasn't. My staff team returned from the conference fired up and loaded with tapes, videos, and books, which they gave to me in the hopes of stirring up my leadership gift. They didn't know it, but their words confirmed my worst suspicions: leaders of large churches are cut out of a different cloth than I am.

One Saturday night I paced before my computer, agonizing over a sermon that refused to be written, the blank screen reflecting the mood of my soul. I called one of my elders. "I'm in trouble, Brother. Help me!" My elders immediately responded. They freed me from all but my pulpit duties for a season and encouraged me to meet with a Christian counselor.

That was a frightening spring. Life blossomed around me, but my inner world was colorless. I couldn't read and couldn't pray. One night after a meeting, I sat in my car for a long time. I couldn't go home because I couldn't remember how to start the car.

The Wisdom of a Tear

On my first visit to the counselor's office I chatted cordially with the receptionist and cracked a joke with my counselor, whom I knew professionally.

"Come in, Doug, have a seat," he said, closing the door. "How are you?"

I wept for most of the next hour. I didn't know why.

Frederick Buechner has written,

Whenever you find tears in your eyes, especially unexpected tears, it is well to pay the closest attention. They are not only telling you something about the secret of who you are, but more often than not God is speaking to you through them of the mystery of where you have come from and summoning you to where, if your soul is to be saved, you should go next.

What were my tears telling me? They were whispering to me the secret of who I was, a thirty-five-year-old spiritually bankrupt pastor who lacked the inner resources to press into his future. My tears also whispered the secret of who I had been. I had been a man of the Book. And that was good. But it was not enough. And so my tears summoned me to where I should go next. They beckoned me to become a man of the Spirit, too. "Our gospel came to you," Paul wrote the Thessalonians, "not simply with words, but also with power" (1 Thess. 1:5). It was time for me to learn how to minister "not simply with words, but also with power."

My tears were ultimately tears of fear. Fear of failing. Fear of impotence. Fear of not having enough in me to finish the race. I thought I would meet with my counselor one time. Instead, we met for over a year. By the end of that time, I learned that those were well-founded fears. I was impotent, and I would fail—unless I learned how to draw so near to Christ that his Spirit drenched everything I did.

I have settled the question of whether or not I am up to the task of leading my church. I am not. But I am going to stay anyway, as long as they'll keep me, because being in over your head is a great way to learn how to live in the Spirit. My quest now is to balance solid orthodoxy with an experiential, intimate walk with Christ. And that's Fellowship's quest, too. I am not alone. Everywhere I go, I am finding Christians who want both intimacy and orthodoxy, both passion and precept. This quest for completeness, I believe, is why churches like Fellowship are growing. Evangelicals and charismatics long for this completeness. Seekers do, too. We want to be whole.

> My tears summoned me to where I should go next. They beckoned me to become a man of the Spirit.

SOME COME FOR TRUTH

A large percentage of Fellowship's congregation is from charismatic churches. They feel at home at here because our worship, our emphasis on prayer, our belief in healing, and our eagerness to hear the voice of God are all part of their tradition. They also come because we care about the cultivation of a Christian mind. They come seeking a biblical worldview to undergird their life in the Spirit.

Gary comes from a large charismatic church in another city. He led a large ministry there and still has many friends in the charismatic movement. Gary's gifts in leading worship and his unique ability to bring a timely word into the toughest of circumstances are skills he developed in the charismatic church. Yet Gary and his family didn't feel complete. "We needed to put down some deeper biblical roots," he explained when asked what God was doing in his life before he came to Fellowship.

SOME COME FOR POWER

Another large percentage of our congregation is from evangelical churches. They feel at home in our church because of our emphasis on expository preaching, our understanding of spiritual growth as more of a journey than an event, and our attempts to build a Christian worldview and to see life through those lenses. They also come because they are drawn to the powerful worship, the opportunity to experience God personally with the expectation of supernatural encounter.

Jan is one of our most effective Bible teachers to women. She has remarkable communication skills and can hold a room captive for an hour with the meatiest of Bible expositions. This type of ministry was satisfying to her—for a while. "I knew there was something more," she recalls. "Christianity had to be more than taking a college course together in Bible."

Jan remains a superb Bible teacher. But now her sessions are woven with opportunities for the Spirit to speak and minister.

SOME COME FOR BOTH

The final portion of the flock wasn't involved much in church before they came to Fellowship. They, too, are drawn to our blend of word and power. This has surprised me and led me to change my thinking about evangelism. I used to think that powerful, expressive worship turned seekers off. Now I am learning that our worship is one of our most powerful evangelistic tools. One seeker told me in tears after a rich worship time, "I don't know what it is. I just sense God here."

Frequently we pray for emotional and physical healing at the end of our services. Several weeks ago, a young man dressed in "alternative" clothing was standing a few feet away from the group receiving prayer. "Can we pray for you?" I asked him. "No," he said. "I'm not really a churchgoer. Thank you anyway."

He stayed where he was, watching people receive prayer. This particular night was uniquely powerful. One of the members of our prayer team who had been praying in the side room during the service (we call it the "prayer cave") had whispered to me, "We sense that there is a woman here tonight with back pain that is caused by a nerve problem on her right side. God wants to touch her tonight." I shared this with the congregation, and instantly a young mother responded. She was in so much pain she could not move her head from right to left. The prayer team laid hands on her, and the pain left. She went to her seat sobbing and holding her husband. Later, I asked her to share what God had done with the congregation. She did, and the congregation gave God a standing ovation.

> When the power is matched with the Word, our guests feel safe.

The young man quietly watched all of this. When the service ended, he came to me and asked, "Can I talk to you?" He was visibly touched by the power of God that night. He wanted to know more about Jesus. I saw him again last Sunday. "This has never happened before," he said. "I really meet with God here."

But power alone would not be enough to attract our nominally churched or unchurched guests. They have a deep suspicion of an overemotional religion, thanks in part to the television evangelist scandals of the eighties. Our power ministry is anchored with the quiet, methodical studying of biblical principles. I teach more like a professor than a televangelist. Our guests are drawn to the power, but afraid of it, too. When the power is matched with the Word, they feel safe.

I want to introduce you to two couples from our congregation who illustrate the quest for completeness found on both sides of the evangelical-charismatic divide.

MARK AND VICKY'S STORY

Mark and Vicky's story will be a familiar one to the thousands of Christians who have been touched by the charismatic renewal. As a junior in high school Mark was nominally involved in a quiet main-line church. Then he met Vicky. Romance was in the wind, marriage and shared ministry were down the road, but God had something else in store first.

Mark noticed something about Vicky's faith that puzzled him. She had a passion for God that he had never encountered before. "She went to this crazy church," he recalls. "My friends told me not to go there because they spoke in tongues and it was all of the devil." Mark ignored his friends' advice and joined Vicky at the high school where her charismatic church met. The service "scared me to death," yet "something was wooing me." Mark stayed with it and soon felt as if he had boarded a flight into a time warp and landed in the book of Acts.

Mark's voice picks up the pace when he begins to recall what happened in those early days. "I saw a deaf girl healed. I knew her personally. I wondered, 'How could this be of the devil?' We saw legs grow—everything! Truly, signs and wonders drew me in." Soon after, Vicky prayed for him to receive the baptism of the Spirit. "My whole body heated up. The Spirit was all over me." Two weeks later, Mark received the gift of tongues. As he tells me these things, Mark's six-foot-five-inch frame shifts back and forth on the padded chair he's sitting on—clearly, these are powerful memories.

"After we were married, we started a prayer group. It exploded—twenty, forty, eighty came out. We had it all—tongues, healings, words of knowledge. I felt like I had gone from death to life."

"People were coming in off the street, getting saved," Vicky recalls. "But something wasn't right. My understanding of the gospel then was, 'Make Jesus your Savior, be baptized in the Spirit, experience his gifts.' We were at church all the time, but . . ."

"We had an unhealthy relationship," Mark adds, finishing Vicky's sentence. "I was abusive to my wife. I was looking at pornography even while my ministry was exploding. Christianity had become one experience after another. I thought the goal was to get people to receive the Baptism. But I wasn't in the Word. The Word was what we were missing."

A series of painful circumstances resulted in their leaving that church and dropping out of church entirely for several years. Eventually Mark and Vicky made their way back to faith, and that way led to our church. Mark began to take in the ministry of the Word and found a depth to his faith he had not known before. He made a commitment to never end a day without spending time in the Scriptures. "That decision changed us forever," he remembers. God released Mark from his anger and his addiction to pornography.

"When Mark made a commitment to be in the Scriptures, that really affected us," Vicky adds. "We began to live holier lives and became consumed with developing our relationship with our Lord."

Mark and Vicky cherish their charismatic tradition. Mark fondly recalls how his relationship with a charismatic pastor here in Knoxville healed a deep wound in his life. Now, however, they are enjoying the best of both worlds. "We were longing to worship God in spirit and in truth," Mark says. "When both come together, it's amazing."

JOHN AND SUE'S STORY

John and Sue come from the other side of the world from Mark and Vicky, geographically and spiritually. John grew up as the child of Baptist missionaries serving in Rhodesia (now Zimbabwe). His father is a graduate of Bob Jones University. John went to boarding school when he was six. He remembers those years as "not unkind" and highly structured, with regular times each day for personal devotions and Bible studies with the dorm parents. John remembers experiencing a spiritual renewal after a motorcycle wreck when he was seventeen. He became obsessed with a hunger to study the Word of God (an obsession that is still with him), and he started rising at 5:30 in the morning to study the Scriptures for an hour and a half.

Sue grew up in Ogden Road Baptist Church in Salisbury (now Harare), Rhodesia. She met John in the church youth group. John married Sue shortly thereafter, and together they forged a faith for their family. At first they joined churches like the ones they grew up in. Yet, too often they found word without power. "We didn't really know God very well in those days," Sue recalls. "There never was a love relationship. I thirsted for relationship, for passion."

A job change landed John and Sue in a small town where there were no Baptist churches. Neighbors invited the young couple to join them at the local Assembly of God church. They reluctantly agreed to go. "We were taught that the gifts had ceased," John says. "There was a time when some of the missionary ladies and some of the boarding school kids began to speak in tongues. That was squashed. We were told it was of the devil." Needless to say, John and Sue were suspicious of their neighbors' Pentecostal church.

"But something real was there," John remembers. "I realized those people would go to heaven with me." Sue agrees, admitting that she is still afraid of the charismatic spiritual gifts, but growing in her understanding of them. She received the gift of tongues one night while praying alone in her bedroom for a friend who was dying with cancer. "It just happened," she recalls. "I wasn't seeking the gift." John never has received the gift of tongues, although he has asked for it.

John and Sue moved to Knoxville and eventually found their way to Fellowship. John began to minister to people wrestling with demonic oppression. His ministry grew until he left his job as a mechanic to devote full-time to his calling.

John smiles as he remembers that a charismatic pastor stated a word of prophecy over him in 1986 that said, "One day God will use you in a healing ministry, helping people find freedom from demonic spirits." The fulfillment of that prophecy awakened John to the Spirit's power and gifts. His ministry became so difficult, he found himself crying out for more spiritual power. "My appreciation for the Spirit's power has come from my own time in the Word, as I searched for help in my ministry," John explains. Today John's ministry is balanced between teaching the Scriptures and praying for the afflicted.

Recently the winds of midlife have rustled up some painful early memories in Sue. "God has used gifts like words of knowledge and visions to set me free, along with his Word," she explains. "I'm finding freedom from a lot of legalism in my past. I hunger for intimacy with God, and I'm finding that as I pursue him in the Spirit and the Word."

Sue and John are becoming whole. "What's going on at Fellowship is similar to Adam receiving Eve to become one," Sue says. "Charismatics and evangelicals really do need each other."

Amen.

STUDY QUESTIONS

1. Have there been ways that your faith has been hindered because of your heritage? Did you experience a spiritual breakdown before realizing it?

2. How can your faith be strengthened by embracing the other tradition?

3. What does your church emphasize more, truth or power? How can you cultivate both in the life of your church?

CHAPTER FOUR

OUR COMMON HERITAGE

G randma Pat passed away last August. We gathered to say good-bye on a fall-like summer Saturday a few blocks away from the white clapboard house that had seen her birth eighty-three years before. Grandma's young minister met with our family for lunch in a quiet hamburger place and did what good pastors do in times like this—he let the family talk.

I will not soon forget the two hours we spent around the table that day. My mom and dad were there, and so were Aunt Marn and Uncle Phil, Cousin Will, and Uncle Frank. Our family is spread all over the country, and I hadn't seen most of my aunts and uncles since I was in high school. (They still call me "Little Dougie." My dad is "Big Doug.") We don't have a tremendous amount in common. We live in different cities, have different careers, and probably believe different things. Yet there was a closeness that day around the table that I have known nowhere else.

When we do come together, my favorite part is hearing about my relatives. I never met most of these people, but I know them— Uncle Hal, whose wooden golf clubs are still in the family cottage, Grandpa Bob, Great Aunt Olive . . . Their stories are my stories. These people are my family. We are joined at a level far deeper than geographical proximity. We come from the same roots. Our unity as a family stems from our common heritage.

Many Christians might be surprised to discover that charismatics and evangelicals also share a common spiritual heritage. We share the same spiritual roots and admire the same heroes. Let's take a moment to page through our family scrapbook. We will find that merging word and power together is more like a far-flung family gathering together again than a shotgun marriage between two unwilling partners.

Charismatics and evangelicals are part of a broad family that is normally referred to as "evangelicalism." Evangelicalism was born during the Protestant Reformation of the sixteenth century when Martin Luther declared that salvation is by grace alone through faith alone, and that the Scriptures are the Christian's only authority. (If you want to impress your pastor, let drop the Latin phrases *sola scriptura* and *sola fide*. These phrases became the watchwords of the Reformation and explain the two main beliefs Luther fought for.)

Alister McGrath, a British theologian, lists six characteristics of evangelicalism:

1. The supreme authority of Scripture.
2. The majesty of Jesus Christ.
3. The Lordship of the Holy Spirit.
4. The need for personal conversion.
5. The priority of evangelism.
6. The importance of Christian community.[1]

Charismatics are clearly evangelicals because they affirm each of these six criteria. The only doctrinal area that separates evangelicals from charismatics is the charismatics' belief that the baptism of the Holy Spirit occurs after conversion. This second work of the Spirit is also called the second blessing.

So if charismatics are evangelicals, then why do we use the terms "charismatic" and "evangelical" to distinguish these two groups? Good question! It doesn't make much sense. Nonetheless, in popular usage, evangelicalism has been divided into two camps—charismatics, who believe in the second blessing, and evangelicals, who do not.

> If charismatics are evangelicals, then why do we use the terms "charismatic" and "evangelical" to distinguish these two groups?

For our purposes, it is important to note that evangelicals and charismatics are both part of the same historical movement known as evangelicalism. Let's take a look now at some of our common ancestors.

THE PIETISTS

The Reformation began well, but didn't end well. A century and a half after Luther nailed the Ninety-five Theses to the castle door at Wittenberg, the Protestant state churches had grown cold and formal. Pietism sought to rekindle the fires of spiritual passion that had burned so brightly so many years earlier.

The Pietists admired the Reformers' emphasis on the study of Scripture. The book that launched the Pietist movement, called *Pious Longings,* begins with this plea: "There should be ... a more extensive use of the Word of God among us."[2] The author, Philip Spener, goes on to argue that listening to good preaching isn't enough—believers need to be in the Word themselves. Sound familiar? The Pietists called these small groups "conventicles." They met on Sunday afternoons to discuss the passage that the pastor preached on that morning. The Pietists were people of the Word.

Yet they also longed to see the head knowledge of the Bible wedded to heart knowledge. They were the first to use the terminology "a personal relationship with Jesus." They saw many in the state churches making a nominal profession of faith but lacking any signs of spiritual life. They called for a personal, experiential relationship with Christ as the only evidence of living faith.

This love affair with Christ was often expressed in their songs. Most hymns of their day sang *about* God. The Pietists wrote love songs *to* Jesus. Pietistic leaders like Nicholas von Zinzendorf described the believer's relationship with God as that of a bride with a groom, and they used sentimental, romantic wording to express feelings of love for Jesus.

Pietists were also eager to listen to the voice of the Spirit speaking through the Scriptures in personal ways. They allowed for the possibility of direct "special revelations" apart from the Bible, but these revelations had to be tested by Scripture. Some of their histories read remarkably like the chronicles of the birth of Pentecostalism. On August 13, 1727, the Holy Spirit fell with such power on a group of Moravian worshipers that they left the church "hardly knowing whether they belonged to earth or had already gone to heaven." The outpouring led to reconciliation in their community, the birth of a hundred-year, around-the-clock prayer vigil, and a renewed vision for world missions. One who was there wrote,

> We read in the Book of Acts many outpourings of the Holy Spirit, as in Samaria, in Ephesus, and even in the case of the Gentiles. Church history also abounds in records of special outpourings of the Holy Ghost, and verily the thirteenth of August, 1727 was a day of outpouring of the Holy Spirit. We saw the hand of God and His wonders and we were all . . . baptized with the Spirit. The Holy Ghost came upon us and in those days great signs and wonders took place in our midst. From that time scarcely a day passed but what we beheld His almighty workings among us. A great hunger for the Word of God took possession of us so that we had to have three services every day. . . . Everyone desired above everything else that the Holy Spirit might have full control. Self-love and self-will as well as all disobedience disappeared and an overwhelming flood of grace swept us all out into the ocean of Divine Love.[3]

A professor friend of mine likes to call himself a "Reformed Pietist." He tries to blend the Reformers' hunger for the Word with the Pietists' thirst for a passionate, personal, powerful faith.

It's not hard to see why evangelicals and charismatics both claim the Pietists as "their own kin."

THE PURITANS

H. L. Mencken described Puritanism as the "haunting fear that someone, somewhere may be happy." Our history books enjoy painting this picture of the dour, joyless Puritans. Read their books, however, and you find a different picture. The Puritans were a passionate people who longed to know their God. The Puritans got their nickname because they wanted to purify Britain's sixteenth-century church. They enjoyed little success, however, and began to immigrate to America in the 1620s, greatly influencing the spiritual soil of the Colonies.

The Puritans loved the Word of God. Earnest listeners brought notebooks to church and used a special shorthand to take copious notes. They turned down the pages of their own Bibles to mark the morning's texts, returning to them after Sunday dinner. They spent much of the rest of their time reading devotional writings that typically took a Scripture verse and applied it to the troubles of the human soul. Puritan devotional writing is among the richest anywhere. "Puritanism was, above all else, a Bible movement."[4] In his classic pastoral guide, *The Reformed Pastor*, the well-known Puritan writer Richard Baxter gives us a glimpse of how his people in the seventeenth century viewed preaching:

> How few ministers preach with all their might.... Alas! We speak so drowsily and softly, that sleeping sinners cannot hear.... What! Speak coldly for God, and for men's salvation?... In the name of God, brethren, labor to awaken your own hearts, before you go into the pulpit, that you may be fit to awaken the hearts of sinners.... Look around upon them with the eye of faith, and with compassion, and think in what a state of joy or torment they must all be forever.... Oh, speak not one cold or careless word about so great a business as heaven or hell.[5]

The Puritans also yearned for the power of the Holy Spirit. John Owen wrote a 651-page work, *A Discourse Concerning the Holy Spirit,* that is still regarded as the most thorough work on this subject in the English language. Puritans also taught that a believer could experience a second blessing, a distinct empowerment of the Spirit long after he had been saved. They called this the "sealing of the Spirit." Modern readers might be surprised to find the Puritan literature full of testimonies about these secondary encounters with the Holy Spirit. They read much like the charismatic testimonies about the Baptism, except that they do not mention speaking in tongues. In the seventeenth century, Puritan theologian Thomas Goodwin called this second work "the electing love of God brought home to the soul" and argued that it was "a distinct thing, a different thing" from conversion.[6] He urged his readers,

> Modern readers might be surprised to find the Puritan literature full of testimonies about secondary encounters with the Holy Spirit.

> There is a special promise, my brethren, unto believers, that they shall have the Spirit to seal them, if they sue it out.... You that are believers, wait for a further promise of the Holy Ghost as sealer, and sue it out with God.[7]

Goodwin, who was also a Cambridge professor, encouraged his congregation, "Let us seek to experience it ourselves."[8] We hear the echoes of these pleas in the sermons of today's Pentecostal and charismatic preachers as they urge their flocks to pursue the baptism with the Holy Spirit.

D. Martyn Lloyd-Jones relates a story that Goodwin used in a sermon to illustrate what this second encounter with the Spirit is like:

A man and his little child [are] walking down the road and they are walking hand in hand, and the child knows that he is a child of his father, and he knows that his father loves him, and he rejoices in that, and he is happy in it. There is no uncertainty about it at all, but suddenly the father, moved by some impulse, takes hold of the child and picks him up, fondles him in his arms, kisses him, embraces him, showers his love upon him, and then he puts him down again and they go on walking together.[9]

Puritanism was a thoroughly biblical movement combined with a passion for what the Puritans called "experimental religion," a faith that touched the heart as well as the head. It is no surprise that evangelicals and charismatics now draw from Puritan writings to support their positions. We can both claim them as "one of us."

JONATHAN EDWARDS

Jonathan Edwards, who shared the Puritan vision, ministered a century later in New England. When the young scholar took over his grandfather's congregation in Northampton, Massachusetts, he found little spiritual vitality. He assaulted the problem with meaty expositions of Scripture and a passionate plea for a faith that could be experienced. His prayers for renewal were answered with the First Great Awakening, which began in 1734. The Awakening was accompanied by the kind of supernatural phenomena currently being experienced in some charismatic renewal services.

Edwards read his sermons through thick glasses in a monotone for fear of bringing the flesh into his preaching. At times his reserved New England parishioners were so struck by his words that they interrupted him with shrieks, sobbing, falling over, and shaking. He discusses these phenomena in detail in his *Faithful Narrative of the Surprising Work of God* and in *The Marks of a Work of the True*

Spirit, concluding that manifestations of the Spirit proved nothing. Enduring spiritual fruit was the sign that a person had been truly touched by the Spirit. He instructed his readers to neither encourage nor discourage these phenomena but to keep the focus on Jesus and watch for fruit. Edwards's treatment of this question is still regarded as the best ever written in English. When the Toronto Blessing broke out in the mid-1990s and evangelicals tried to make sense of it, they reprinted Edwards's teaching on the subject.

> It is no surprise that Jonathan Edwards's writings are often cited in support of both the evangelical and charismatic movements.

Edwards is a towering figure from church history who was so skilled in the study of Scripture that he is regarded as America's greatest theologian while also having a burning desire for a faith that stirred the affections. He championed careful exposition of Scripture and openness to the Spirit's power. It is no surprise that Edwards's writings are often cited in support of both the evangelical and charismatic movements.

JOHN WESLEY, CHARLES FINNEY, AND D. L. MOODY

John Wesley was the son of a stern Anglican pastor, the fifteenth of nineteen children. His life and ministry spanned nearly a century (1703–1791) and brought renewal to a dry and intellectual British Christianity. Wesley hoped to stay within the Anglican Church but was ultimately forced out. Methodism was born, dramatically transforming England and then spilling onto the shores of America to do the same.

Wesley, who was eventually banned from Anglican pulpits, devised an evangelistic strategy known as revivalism. He was the first to take the gospel to the masses, preaching sermons three times a day anywhere he could draw a crowd. His followers brought this method to America, and the Methodist camp meeting brought thousands to Christ on the American frontier.

Wesley's revivalism eventually put its stamp on much of American evangelicalism. The Billy Graham Crusades, Southern Baptist revival meetings, and Pentecostal tent revivals all trace their roots back to Wesley. Evangelicals are fond of remembering that Wesley was a brilliant theologian who put the most complex of subjects into the language of the common man. Charismatics point out that the supernatural phenomena experienced in their revival meetings often pale in comparison to what Wesley experienced in his. Wesley once wrote in his journal, "Many, no doubt, were . . . struck down, both body and soul, into the depth of distress."[10] John Cennick, one of Wesley's preaching associates, tells us,

> One night more than twenty roared and shrieked together while I was preaching . . . [some of whom] confessed they were demoniacs. . . . I have seen people so foam and violently agitated that six men could not hold one, but he would spring out of their arms or off the ground, and tear himself in hellish agonies. Others I have seen sweat uncommonly, and their necks and tongues swell and twist out of all shape.[11]

Wesley's theology of the second blessing eventually paved the way for charismatic second-blessing theology. He believed in two distinct works of grace in the believer's life. The second work of grace would significantly help believers deal with sin and walk in new power. Charles Finney, the great American evangelist, took this idea and developed it, preaching a similar doctrine at Oberlin College in the 1830s. Finney experienced this baptism himself, and described it like this:

> The Holy Spirit descended upon me in a manner that seemed to go through me, body and soul. I could feel the impression, like a wave of electricity, going through and through me. Indeed it seemed to come in waves and waves of liquid love. . . . It seemed like the very breath of God. . . . I wept aloud with joy and love; and I do not know but I should say, I literally bellowed out the unutterable gushings of my heart. These waves came over me, and over me, and over me, one after the other, until I recollect I cried out, "I shall die if these waves continue to pass over me." I said, "Lord, I cannot bear any more."[12]

Finney has had a profound influence on evangelicals and charismatics. Baptists owe their method of altar call directly to Finney. He was the first to attempt it and was so successful that it became a staple of American revivalism. Charismatics owe their theology of the second blessing to Finney, who picked it up where Wesley left off and held onto it until it became part of the theological landscape of late nineteenth-century evangelicalism.

Prominent evangelists D. L. Moody and R. A. Torrey taught the doctrine at the end of the nineteenth century, encouraging their audiences to seek the baptism of the Holy Ghost. It is not hard to see how Pentecostalism sprung forth from the fertile second-blessing soil tilled by the preaching of these great evangelists.

Today Moody's name stands for the very best of evangelicalism—Moody Bible Institute, Moody Publishing, the great Moody Memorial Church in Chicago. Yet charismatics can claim him, too. His influence and writings on the Baptism, perhaps more than any other person, gave birth to the very movement that evangelicals have so long feared as coming from the devil!

THE KESWICK MOVEMENT

The Keswick movement emerged in Britain in the late nineteenth century. Keswick teaching is named after the doctrines presented in a weeklong tent meeting held in the scenic Lake District site of Keswick, beginning in 1875. Keswick teachers believed the spiritual life to be distinguished in two distinct stages. The first stage is characterized by spiritual defeat. The second phase is marked by victory over sin. Believers enter the second stage through a spiritual crisis. Keswick teachers did not call this crisis a second blessing but described it as entering into the fullness of the Spirit. Believers experienced this fullness when they surrendered all to Christ.

Evangelicals find a gallery of their most prominent spiritual grandparents leading the Keswick meetings. Conference platforms featured the likes of Hudson Taylor, Andrew Murray, Amy Carmichael, Handley Moule, F. B. Meyer, G. Campbell Morgan, and D. L. Moody. Robert McQuilken, a Keswick disciple, founded Columbia School of the Bible, which became an evangelical outpost of Keswick teaching, while C. I. Scofield wove Keswick teachings into his famous Scofield Reference Bible and later into the curriculum of the Bible school that became Dallas Theological Seminary. The most popular Keswick teacher of our day is Stephen Olford. His latest book has a foreword by the dean of evangelicals, Billy Graham.

Charismatics can hang the portraits of many of these great leaders on their walls as well. Andrew Murray, whose devotional writings are cherished by evangelicals and are still best-sellers, also wrote a book called *Spiritual Excellence* that flatly states,

> In these chapters it is my desire to bring to the children of God the message that there is a two-fold Christian life. The one is that in which we experience something of the operations of the Holy Spirit . . . but we do not receive Him as the Pentecostal Spirit, as the personal indwelling guest. On the other hand, there is a more abundant life, in which the indwelling just referred to is known and experienced. . . . this gift is something quite different from conversion.[13]

Murray wrote these words just two decades before Pentecostalism was born. Evangelicals have been shaped by Murray's warm insights about the abundant Christian life. Charismatics can trace their doctrine of the second blessing back to him as well.

The Keswick teachers stressed the possibility of the victorious Christian life and the need for a definitive crisis experience. Evangelicals went on to downplay the "crisis" aspect of the experience; Pentecostals and charismatics tended to play it up. Yet both camps owe much of their present theology to the Keswick teachers who unfolded the Scriptures for sweating saints on a British conference ground a century and a quarter ago.

D. MARTYN LLOYD-JONES

D. Martyn Lloyd-Jones was the influential pastor of London's Westminster Chapel from 1939 to 1968. He is often referred to as "the greatest preacher of this century." His careful, detailed expository sermons, delivered with steely passion and compelling logic, did much to elevate the primacy of preaching on both sides of the Atlantic when liberalism was dominating the most fashionable pulpits. Few preachers have influenced evangelical pastors more than Lloyd-Jones. His sermons on Romans, Ephesians, and the Sermon on the Mount are now classics, and you can find them in nearly every evangelical pastor's library. Preaching was the center of his ministry, the passion of his life. Evangelicals salute him for rescuing the pulpit from the challenge of liberalism.

> Both camps owe much of their present theology to the Keswick teachers who unfolded the Scriptures a century and a quarter ago.

Charismatics salute Lloyd-Jones as well, for he was the first respected evangelical to challenge the doctrine of cessation. He firmly believed in a baptism of the Spirit that followed conversion. Long before John Wimber started the Vineyard movement, "the Doctor" (as Lloyd-Jones was affectionately called due to his medical training) was arguing that signs and wonders were a means to awaken a secular world to the gospel. Ironically, a charismatic known for his expository preaching gifts fills the Doctor's former pulpit today.

↳↗

A yellowed photograph hangs on the wall in the dining room of my grandmother's summer cottage. I believe it was taken in the fall of 1917. People didn't smile for pictures back then, and this shot is typical. A dozen or so elderly folk, many of whom are my relatives, stand on the front porch of the cottage and gaze somberly at the photographer. Inked on the bottom of the picture is the phrase, "The Lingerlongers." This was the nickname for this bunch, because they lingered longer on the island than any of the other vacationers.

The people in that picture have been gazing over my family for almost a hundred years. They watched over my dad when he ate Wheaties there as a little boy. They watched over me. Now they keep an eye on my kids, too. I think of that picture sometimes, when life seems disconnected and lonely, and I wonder where I belong. The Lingerlongers remind me of who I am, of where I have been, and where I hope to go. Family snapshots do that for you—if you let them.

I hope this quick tour of evangelicalism's family album has brought us closer together as a spiritual family. We share a common heritage, common heroes, and for the most part, a common theology. Best of all, we are a family.

↳↗

Note: If your church's tradition is charismatic, it may be more beneficial to study chapter 6 before chapter 5 so that you can first cherish your own tradition and then appreciate the other.

STUDY QUESTIONS _____

1. Does your church accept the six characteristics of evangelicalism? If so, what are the implications of knowing that churches of the other tradition do, too?

2. Are you surprised to discover that the two traditions share so many of the same "ancestors"? Discuss. Does that fact draw you closer to the other tradition?

3. Discuss Goodwin's story of a child walking with his father. Does this analogy touch you? Do you desire both the steady walk and the intimate touch?

4. Your spiritual ancestors embraced both traditions simultaneously. What are some specific ways your church can move back to this balanced view?

CHAPTER FIVE

THE LEGACY OF EVANGELICALS

I knew I loved Dr. Rosscup the first time I met him. It was August. It was Los Angeles. And it was hot. Seventy of us wiped drops of sweat off our faces and flipped through our newly purchased syllabi waiting for our first seminary course to begin. The course was Hermeneutics: How to Study the Bible. This, we had all been told, was the heart of the curriculum at the Talbot School of Theology. Dr. James Rosscup—scholar of international repute, writer of western novels (under the pen name Jim Ross), and owner of two earned doctorates—didn't just teach the course. He *was* the course. He had been teaching Talbot students Bible study methods for twenty years. Students both feared and loved him.

Dr. Rosscup walked in, as was his custom, a minute before the hour. He set down a rumpled satchel full of books and notes by his lectern, smiled, and began my seminary education. Look up the word *scholar* in the dictionary, and you might well see a picture of Dr. Rosscup. Eleven years of graduate school had robbed him of most of his hair. Thick black glasses that reminded you of—well, glasses seminary professors might wear—perched on the end of his nose as he would ponder his notes, both hands firmly gripping his lectern, sweat stains soiling a crisp white button-down shirt.

"I'm not going to lecture today," he began on that sweltering August morning in 1984. "I just want to share with you my testimony." For an hour we sat, spellbound in sweaty seats, listening to the story of a man for whom the Word was life and life was the Word. His had not been an easy path. The migraine headaches that had tormented him through the years were exceptionally terrible when he was studying for his first doctorate. He would come home from spending hours in the Scriptures, his head throbbing, and place his head in his wife's lap and have her pray for him.

Another doctoral program took Dr. Rosscup to Scotland. He then went back to his first love: teaching Bible. I have never met a man who knew the Word the way he did. What amazed me, though, was not his Bible knowledge but how that knowledge shaped his soul.

Dr. Rosscup's wife was bedridden with a painful disease. She had been in that condition for many years and, as far as I know, remained that way for many more. Dr. Rosscup's love for his wife was as deep and pure as a Scottish loch. His faithfulness to her was born out of a sacred romance that the young will never understand and the old rarely do. He didn't just *endure* her sickness; he passionately loved her in the midst of it. Often, in the middle of a lecture (perhaps on the seven possibilities of who the *nephilim* are in Genesis 6), he would pause and share a tender word about his wife.

Once he read a love poem he had written to her. It was not a poem composed in the spring of their love when sickness had not yet stolen some of their freedom. It was a poem penned in the autumn of their passion when lesser couples let love die.

When I think of Dr. Rosscup, I think of Psalm 1:

> Blessed is the man who does not walk in the counsel of the wicked or stand in the way of sinners or sit in the seat of mockers. But his delight is in the law of the LORD, and on his law he meditates day and night. He is like a tree planted by streams of water, which yields its fruit in season and whose leaf does not wither. Whatever he does prospers.

CELEBRATE WHO YOU ARE, EMBRACE WHO YOU CAN BECOME

Some books in my library are written from evangelicals to charismatics. Their goal is to show the charismatics that they are wrong and to persuade them to change. Some books in my library are written from charismatics to evangelicals. Their goal is to show the evangelicals that they are wrong and to persuade them to change. This book isn't like that.

This book is not asking you to give up who you are. I could never give up the richness of my heritage, the cherished memories of hours spent under the teaching of men like Dr. Rosscup. This book asks you to rejoice in who you are and then calls you to become even better. Both the charismatic and the evangelical traditions bring with them a rich legacy that deserves to be embraced. We become word and power churches not by letting go of our own legacy, but by embracing the strengths brought by the other tradition.

> We become word and power churches not by letting go of our own legacy, but by embracing the strengths brought by the other tradition.

This chapter will survey five gifts evangelicals bring to today's church. The following chapter will survey five gifts charismatics bring to today's church. Word and power churches embrace all ten of these strengths. (By singling out these gifts, I am not implying that the other camp has no gifting in that regard. Rather, I am suggesting that these are the "specialty areas" in which God has allowed each tradition to excel.)

EXPOSITORY PREACHING PROCLAIMS THE WORD OF GOD

My introduction to expository preaching came from one of the masters: Chuck Swindoll, pastor of the First Evangelical Free Church in Fullerton, California. The church I served in before seminary did not have a Sunday evening service, so my wife and I would slip away and sit under the ministry of one of the twentieth century's greatest expository preachers. My life began to change. My hunger for the Scriptures became insatiable. The worship service became a delicious meal after a week spent dining on fast food. My passion for the Lord was stirred. I was benefiting from the ministry of expository preaching.

God gives teachers to his church to help the body of Christ mature (Eph. 4:11). Evangelicals have championed expository preaching as a highly effective way to proclaim the Word of God. Expository sermons have three characteristics:

1. Expository preaching is God-centered. Teachers enter their study asking, "Father, what do you want to say to the flock this week?" rather than, "Father, I've got a few things on my mind I want to teach on. Can you help me find a text to back them up?" Teachers who take the latter approach are limited to their own experiences and preferences, and their congregations are not fed the whole counsel of God. Many expositional preachers prefer verse-by-verse preaching through books of the Bible for just this reason—it forces them to cover everything in the Bible, not just their pet topics. For example, if I had not been committed to verse-by-verse preaching, I am sure I never would have preached on 1 Corinthians 12 and been challenged to change my views. I have been amazed over the years to see God's timing as to where we were in a particular book with our needs as a congregation.

2. Expository preaching is text-focused. One of the great doctrines of the Reformation is the clarity of Scripture. This means that the Bible's teachings can be understood by ordinary believers. A good expository sermon explains the text so thoroughly that listeners can read the text on their own and understand it.

The pastor of the church I attended in seminary was a great Bible expositor. Each Sunday he would carefully explain the meaning of the text and impress it upon our minds and hearts. When I would return to the passage later in the week, I could understand the text for myself.

We can clearly understand Scripture by applying some basic guidelines. Here are several time-honored Bible-study principles:

- Study the passage in context.
- Find out what the words meant in the original language.
- Study the grammar so you understand how the passage flows together.
- Consider the historical background of the passage.
- Study cross-references that address the same subject.
- Compare your conclusions with what other respected teachers have said.

The bottom line is, "If the plain sense makes good sense, seek no other sense!"

The process of applying these Bible study principles is called *exegesis*. The Greek preposition *ex* means "out of." The goal of exegesis is to draw *out of* the text its original meaning. Preachers try to discover what the passage meant to the original audience. They need to be careful when they craft their sermons to make sure that they show their listeners why the text means what it does. If preachers fail to do this, the authority of the sermon rests in them and not in the Word. Good expositors let the text speak for itself.

Text-centered preaching is vital to a healthy pulpit ministry, because it is God's inspired Word that changes lives, not a pastor's opinions or favorite stories. The test of a good expository sermon is this: Did the Scripture impact the hearers the most, or did the preacher's jokes, emotion, or stories? If it is the latter, the power of the sermon has been lost. The best expository sermons leave the hearer remembering the very words of the passage itself, as if Christ had spoken them afresh.

Some preaching today tends to focus on the hidden meaning, the esoteric interpretation. Teachers amaze the audience by pulling principles out of texts that no one else sees. Usually the reason why no one else sees the principle is because it isn't really there. Groups where this kind of preaching prevails often develop cryptic language that the "uninitiated" don't understand. This comes dangerously close to the heresy of gnosticism that dogged the early church. The Gnostics believed that "true believers" could understand veiled, higher truths that everyone else could not. One's ability to discern these mysterious higher truths became the measure of spirituality.

> Text-centered preaching is vital to a healthy pulpit ministry, because it is God's inspired Word that changes lives.

This error often occurs in churches that have a strong prophetic tradition. The prophetic ministry, as we will see in a later chapter, is subjective. A word of prophecy does not bear the authority of Scripture and is not an explanation of Scripture. A prophecy is an impression, placed in the heart by God for the body of Christ or someone in the body. By contrast, the teaching ministry is objective. The teacher's goal is to correctly handle the Word and proclaim it clearly (2 Tim. 2:15). We need to be careful not to blur the distinction between the prophetic ministry and the teaching ministry. Sermons that are long on hidden meanings may in fact have more prophetic content than teaching. A congregation needs to know the difference.

One preacher noted that the book of Revelation mentions an eagle. "The eagle stands for the United States!" he continued. "The United States will fly like an eagle." But the churches John was writing to in the first century A.D. would not have understood the eagle to mean the United States. Perhaps the preacher had a prophetic word about the future of our country. He should have identified it as such.

3. Expository preaching is application-driven. The evangelical tradition places so much emphasis on rightly dividing the text and determining its original meaning that some preachers forget to apply it! Evangelical pastors often have such a love for study that they forget that not everyone is blessed by a ten-minute word study on sin.

Preachers are only halfway done with their task when they have accurately interpreted the passage. The final step is to bridge the gap between the first century and our own. Some fear that preaching verse by verse through a book of the Bible is bound to be academic and boring. But it need not be. Rick Warren of Saddleback Church in California is one of the nation's premier teachers and is uniquely gifted at applying Bible passages to the needs of modern life. He suggests treating each section in the book as an independent unit and then wrapping it in a user-friendly format that is highly application-oriented. I have been preaching through the gospel of Matthew and have been applying Warren's method to my sermon preparation. Most passages answer pressing, felt-need issues, like "how to cope with loneliness" or "how to make sense of suffering." I try to discover the one main truth in the passage and then ask, "To what need in the congregation does this speak to?" Then I build the sermon around meeting that need.

Pastors and congregations who want to benefit from expository preaching can profit from several simple steps.

- Do away with the misguided notion that scholarship is unspiritual. Anti-intellectualism is not a Christian virtue. Why do we accept the evangelist and the prophet, but not the teacher? The church's teachers, professors, and authors are God's gifts to the church. Word and power churches have a healthy value for theological education and advanced biblical training.
- Congregations, give your pastor the time and the resources to prepare. The Jerusalem elders had the right priorities: "We . . . will devote ourselves to prayer and to serving of the word" (Acts 6:4 NRSV). "Pay close attention to . . . your teaching," Paul told young Timothy (1 Tim. 4:16 NRSV). Expository preaching takes a lot of work. Allow your pastor a minimum of twelve hours a week to study and prepare. Give him a book allowance so he can have the tools he needs to do the job well.

- Pastors, don't substitute the leading of the Spirit for the sweaty discipline of sitting down each week and carefully, prayerfully studying the chosen passage. Study, then let the Spirit lead. We must not let our conviction that God speaks directly to us become an excuse for not paying the price of careful Bible study.
- Clarify the difference between the teaching gift and the prophetic gifts. Encourage your congregation to be receptive to both. Prophecy is spontaneous. Teaching is most often carefully prepared.
- Beware of the novel or sensational interpretation. Paul warns us that "the time will come when they will not endure sound doctrine; but wanting to have their ears tickled, they will accumulate for themselves teachers according to their own desires; and will turn away their ears from the truth" (2 Tim. 4:3–4 NASB). People by nature are faddish and look for something new.

Expository preachers must resist the temptation to have to shock their congregations with novel interpretations. The goal of expository teaching is not to deliver a new message, but to faithfully bring forth an old one: the faith once delivered to the saints. Great preaching is creative, fresh, and spiritually sensitive to today's needs. The secret lies in learning to bring a classic, historic truth in a vibrant, compelling way. The rule of thumb is this: Be creative with the application, not the principle. Principles never change. Application always does.

"The primary task of the Church," D. Martyn Lloyd-Jones reminds us, "is to preach and to proclaim [the Word], to show man's real need, and to show the only remedy, the only cure for it."[1]

> The secret of great preaching lies in learning to bring a classic, historic truth in a vibrant, compelling way.

SCRIPTURE HAS ALL AUTHORITY

Last winter I had the opportunity to visit the city of Worms, Germany, where Martin Luther was tried for heresy in 1521. The ancient brick church that housed the trial still stands quietly in the center of the town, its secrets silenced by the sounds of nearby traffic and teenagers skateboarding a few yards away. Behind the church is an enormous statue of the Reformer. Luther's famous reply to Rome's demand that he recant his teaching is written on a rusty bronze plaque fixed to the monument:

> Unless I am convicted by Scripture and plain reason—I do not accept the authority of popes and councils, for they have contradicted each other—my conscience is captive to the Word of God. I cannot and I will not recant anything, for to go against conscience is neither right nor safe. God help me. Here I stand. I cannot do otherwise.

Scripture was Luther's sole authority. Before long, *sola scriptura* became the battle cry of the Reformation. Simply put, the doctrine of the authority of Scripture means that God's Word is fully sufficient for all of faith and practice and has binding authority over the believer. Luther's translation of the Bible into German and the invention of the printing press combined to place the Scripture in the hands of the laypeople for the first time in history. Evangelicals from then on have been a people of the Book, living under the Book.

This commitment to the authority of Scripture was boldly challenged in the early years of the twentieth century as liberal scholars questioned the historical reliability of the Bible. Could the Bible be trusted? Should it have ultimate authority in the believer's life? Evangelicals rose to the challenge and answered "Yes!" Men like J. Gresham Machen of Princeton Seminary defended the trustworthiness of the Bible against modernist attacks. A Southern California millionaire funded the publication of *The Fundamentals*, a twelve-volume defense of the Bible's authority, written by the leading Bible teachers of the time and published from 1910 to 1915.

Seminaries and Bible institutes were launched, committed to forging a Christian worldview that was intellectually honest and faithful to the scriptural authority. During the forties and fifties, the great evangelical parachurch movements began. Campus Crusade, Youth for Christ, Young Life, InterVarsity, the Navigators, and numerous other groups called the nation's young people to the personal study of Scripture and regular memorization of Scripture. Today the authority of Scripture remains a given in evangelical churches, thanks in large part to the faithful work of such men and movements as these.

Word and power churches embrace the authority of Scripture with the same intensity Luther brought to the Diet of Worms. What does this commitment mean practically in our churches?

1. There are no shortcuts. We cannot bypass the spiritual discipline of careful, prayerful study and memorization of the Bible day by day, week by week, year after year. When I first experienced some of the charismatic gifts and found that God really did speak today, I was tempted to place too much emphasis on hearing from God through these gifts. After all, studying the Bible is hard work! Why take the time and energy if God can just speak to me directly? I soon realized that the revelatory gifts were no substitute for the study of Scripture. Eventually I discovered that it is often in an environment where Scripture is being faithfully studied that the revelatory gifts have the most impact.

A woman told me her story, one filled with tragedy, failure, and pain. Her life was a disaster, and many of her wounds were self-inflicted. I was surprised to hear the woman refer often to the many ways the Lord speaks to her. Her life, it seemed, had been one charismatic experience after another, filled with dramatic prophecies and words from the Lord.

"Do you ever read the Bible?" I asked.

"No," she replied. She had failed to balance the prophetic gifts with a life grounded in the Word of God. And she was paying the price for it.

2. The Scriptures must be central in worship services. Prophetic words have a place in public worship, but they must never replace the Scriptures as the central source of authority. The revelatory gifts have less authority than the written Word. When a church spends more energy responding to prophetic words than understanding and obeying the clear words of Scripture, the congregation is in danger of spinning out of control. Scripture is the North Star by which all the gifts set their compasses. We forget this to our peril.

"I loved my church," one man told me. "But I was forced to take my family and leave. Over time, there was less and less teaching and more and more times where we just 'heard from the Lord.' I can't grow on that."

3. We must teach people how to think within a Christian worldview. The Reformers used the Latin phrase *coram Deo*, which means "before God," to describe what it means to live under a Christian worldview. To live under the authority of Scripture is to live under the authority of God. One of the great challenges of discipleship is learning to think with a Christian perspective about all of life.

We must know more than isolated proof texts from the Bible. We must know what the whole Bible teaches about any given subject, and then we must think through how to apply that teaching to our lives today. How do I live in the market place *coram Deo?* Do my personal financial decisions reflect my belief that I live under the authority of God? What type of lifestyle is appropriate for me if I truly live *coram Deo?* How should I relate to a culture that seems to be morally disintegrating—do I run away, jump in, take over?

At no other time in this nation's history have the values of popular culture been so radically at odds with the values of the kingdom of God. We need to help people think critically about what they believe and why they believe it.

I recently had the opportunity of leading my friend Jim to Christ. We meet for several hours each Saturday to study the Scriptures together. Our goal during these times is to build within Jim "the mind of Christ," a way of thinking biblically about all of life. Jim is the CEO of a major corporation. He is learning how to run his business *coram Deo,* and it is enjoyable and rewarding to watch it happen. Together we wrestle with a scriptural approach to profit margins and personnel issues, organizational theory and our responsibility to the poor.

4. We must let Scripture have authority over our feelings. The ultimate test of truth for a Christian living under the authority of Scripture is "What does the Bible say?" and not "What do I feel?" Feelings are important, but they are not a reliable, final test for truth.

> The doctrine of biblical authority teaches us to submit all of life, including our feelings, to the reign of God.

Some Christians seem to go from experience to experience, always yearning for the next spiritual high. I have been in revival services where the preaching and worship seemed almost incidental to the ministry time at the end. I have met with people who feel they are called by God to minister and want to know if it is proper to leave their wife and kids to obey the call!

The doctrine of biblical authority teaches us to submit all of life, including our feelings, to the reign of God.

THE KINGDOM OF GOD IS NOT FULLY HERE

Few topics in Scripture are as puzzling as the kingdom of God. Sometimes Jesus says the kingdom of God *is* here. His primary message was, "Repent, for the kingdom of heaven is near" (Matt. 4:17). When he cast out demons, he said it was proof that "the kingdom of God has come upon you" (Matt. 12:28). Yet Jesus also acknowledged that in some sense the kingdom was *not yet* here. Caesar was still on the throne. Children still starved. Beggars still pleaded for crumbs. And the King still had to die.

Bible scholars have coined a phrase to describe the mystery of the kingdom. They say the kingdom is "already but not yet." Jesus did bring in the kingdom at his first coming. He dealt a decisive death blow to Satan at the cross. The kingdom of God truly did invade the earth. The kingdom in this sense is already here: Eternity has broken into time. But the kingdom is also not yet here. We live between the ages, between the first and the second comings of the Messiah. The full presence of the kingdom awaits Christ's return.

Theologian Oscar Cullman compares this ambiguity about the kingdom to the period in World War II between D-Day and VE-Day. From D-Day on, it was clear that the Allies had defeated Germany. Yet many months of bloody fighting and strategic operations remained before the war was finally over.[2]

Evangelicals remind us of the "not yet" dimension of the kingdom. Scripture reminds us that we live in a fallen world. Paul laments that "the whole creation has been groaning as in the pains of childbirth" (Rom. 8:22). The world groans under Adam's curse. The effects of that curse have not yet been fully lifted. Paul knew all too well the bitter taste of living in a fallen world. He uses words like "crushed" and "perplexed" to capture the pain he felt as he battled the chaos of life, even coming to the point of saying, "Death is at work in us, but life is at work in you" (2 Cor. 4:12).

Suffering is inevitable in a fallen world. We are not promised a life free of problems. We are promised the strength and courage to face our problems with hope. Even Jesus "learned obedience from what he suffered" (Heb. 5:8).

Ken Gire wrote, "The closest communion with God comes, I believe, through the sacrament of tears. Just as grapes are crushed to make wine and grain to make bread, so the elements of this sacrament come from the crushing experiences of life."[3]

Evangelicals remind us that there will be tears and that in these tears we can meet God.

During the eighties there was a great debate about "power evangelism"—that is, evangelism attested by signs and wonders. When people see the power of God at work in their lives through miraculous gifts, the argument goes, they will be encouraged to trust in Christ. I believe this. The loud power of the supernatural does reveal the glory of God to the lost.

But I also believe quiet power does, too. By quiet power I mean the miracle of peace by a graveside, the miracle of a divorcee's forgiving heart, the miracle of moral purity in a sin-stained world. Grasping the not-yet nature of the kingdom helps us look for the quiet power of God in suffering and reminds us that this is not our home.

SPIRITUAL GROWTH IS A PROCESS

Eugene Peterson once titled a book, *A Long Obedience in the Same Direction.*[4] That's a pretty fair description of the Christian life.

Much of the charismatic literature on the Christian life is event-oriented. Testimonies often center on the crisis event of the baptism of the Spirit or a particular deliverance or divine encounter. *Charisma* magazine, for example, advertises dozens of conferences believers can choose from to bolster their spiritual growth. Evangelical literature, by contrast, describes the Christian life as more of a journey than an event. Contrast, for example, John Sherrill's *They Speak with Other Tongues* with John Bunyan's *Pilgrim's Progress.*

God does use significant events in our lives. But a crisis-driven spirituality that depends too heavily on the next event will not sustain a lifetime of spiritual growth. Sometimes believers can become addicted to crisis-events, rushing from church to church or conference to conference in search of the next touch from God.

Dallas Willard makes the wise observation that often those who are blessed with a dramatic spiritual crisis have prepared themselves by faithfully walking on the Christian journey day after day, year after year. "There is no quick fix for the human condition," he cautions. "The approach to wholeness is for humankind a process of great length and difficulty that engages all our own powers to their fullest extent over a long course of experience. But we don't like to hear this."[5]

Paul describes his own journey with sweaty, vigorous words: "Forgetting what is behind and straining toward what is ahead, I press on toward the goal to win the prize" (Phil. 3:13–14). Pressing on is hard work. God is at work in us, Paul says (Phil. 2:13), but *we* must "make every effort ... to be holy" (Heb. 12:14). We must "cleanse ourselves" (2 Cor. 7:1 NASB) and "make every effort" to grow spiritually (2 Peter 1:5). Evangelicals guard us from opting for a drive-through, quick-fix spirituality by reminding us that spiritual growth is ultimately "a long obedience in the same direction."

SMALL GROUPS RENEW THE CHURCH

Neither evangelicals nor charismatics can claim the small group as their exclusive contribution to the church. Small groups have been around since Jesus started one with some Galilean fishermen. Since the Reformation, small groups have played a vital role in renewing the church. The Pietists made them the center of their strategy to renew the churches of Western Europe. John Wesley's ministry left behind a powerful movement while the influence of his peer and fellow evangelist George Whitefield faded with his death. Why? Wesley placed his people into small groups while Whitefield did not.

> Neither evangelicals nor charismatics can claim the small group as their exclusive contribution to the church.

Evangelicals and charismatics have used small groups for different purposes. Charismatics have found the small group a perfect climate for prayer and ministry in the charismatic gifts, while evangelicals have found the small group a great place for accountability and the study of the Scriptures. Word and power churches expect that both benefits will result from the small group.

I have been in small groups of the evangelical variety for nearly all of my Christian life. We have met in locker rooms, fraternities, hotels, and swimming pools, on the beach, and in the back rooms of businesses. A few have been boring. Some have been revolutionary. Most have been good. And the Scriptures have been at the center of each one.

The evangelical parachurch groups have been especially skilled at training their disciples in small-group environments. A whole generation of adults who were discipled by parachurch groups in the sixties, seventies, and eighties now see small-group Bible study as one of the core strategies for spiritual growth.

Why are small groups so well suited to the study and application of the Bible? Because they allow students to question, restate, disagree, and debate, all of which enhance the learning process. The small-group environment also allows for accountability. Group members can share how the text has impacted them and ask for support as they work the truths into everyday life. Few things are a better incentive to holiness than knowing that your small group is going to check up on you next Thursday night.

Word and power churches place a great priority on the preaching of the Word. But preaching alone is not enough. Jesus modeled for us the small group as the best means for making disciples. Word and power churches are small-group driven, gathering their people together to study the Word.

SUMMARY

These five building blocks—expository preaching, the authority of Scripture, the mystery of the kingdom, spiritual growth as a process, and spiritual renewal through small groups—are the legacy of the evangelical church. If they are already in place in your church, thank God. If they are not, begin to weave them into the life of your fellowship. But don't stop there. The next chapter unfolds five more gifts that are the legacy of the charismatic church. Word and power churches embrace the best of both traditions and build their ministries on all ten of the building blocks discussed in these chapters.

STUDY QUESTIONS

1. Can you see the wisdom in "rejoicing in who you are and then becoming even better"? Why is it important to spend time cherishing your own heritage?

2. Discuss the strengths of the evangelical church:
   A. Expository preaching proclaims the Word of God
   B. Scripture has all authority
   C. The kingdom of God is not fully here
   D. Spiritual growth is a process
   E. Small groups renew the church

3. In which areas does your church excel? How can your church grow in the areas in which it is weak?

Chapter Six

THE LEGACY OF THE CHARISMATICS

I am embarrassed to admit how narrow-minded and prideful I have been at times about who knows what in the body of Christ. There was a time when I suspected that charismatics were dubious Christians at best, hopelessly deceived at worst. I found a twisted sense of power criticizing them from my pulpit.

Then I started to meet some of the people I had been criticizing. I was surprised to find that these supposed enemies of mine were actually dear brothers and sisters in Christ who knew many things about God I didn't know.

One of the first charismatic believers to upset my theological applecart was my brother-in-law, Joe. Joe is a gentle giant of a guy—six-foot-seven—who left a tremendous evangelical church in southern California to join John Wimber in the growing Vineyard movement. Joe met Sharon, my wife Sandi's sister, about the same time I began dating Sandi. I remember being very concerned about this nefarious influence in my potential family-to-be. We had been witnessing to Sharon, and I didn't want to see the seed stolen away by a charismatic!

Nothing ruins a good stereotype better than actually meeting the person you have been caricaturing. That's what happened when I began to get to know Joe. It didn't help that he was a kind, gentle, balanced man. Even worse, he seemed to experience God in ways I didn't. True, there were some areas I was strong in where he wasn't, but he seemed to know a side of the Christian life to which I hadn't even been exposed.

Shortly after Joe and I married the sisters, we spent a weekend on the Colorado River together. I was in the middle of my seminary training at the time, and Joe was involved in the signs-and-wonders movement, then in its infancy. Late one sweltering desert evening we were talking theology in our in-law's boat when it hit me: This guy really loves the Lord. And I can learn from him.

Eventually Joe learned to put up with me, too. He is now the worship pastor at Fellowship Church.

Joe never asked me to change. He always expressed respect and appreciation for my evangelical strengths. What he did do over the years was quietly reveal to me another side of walking with Jesus. His example called me not to abandon my heritage, but to broaden my knowledge of God. I am glad I decided to learn from Joe.

The charismatic legacy is a rich one. Let's consider five gifts the charismatic movement has given to the church.

PRAYER IS ESSENTIAL

Everybody prays. But the charismatic movement especially has strengthened the church's prayer life and has given greater priority and energy to prayer than many evangelical churches. We are currently enjoying a growing prayer movement in our city. Recently more than fifty pastors from a wide variety of traditions met together for a four-day Prayer Summit. This was the first time anything like this has happened in our town, which has a reputation for division among its churches. The Spirit met us powerfully in the Summit, tearing down relational walls, bringing about unity, and giving us a shared vision for the city. Now pastor prayer cells are springing up all over the community. The movement began when several charismatic brothers who had been praying together invited several evangelical pastors to pray with them.

I have been asked to provide leadership to the local prayer movement. Part of that task has been to meet with other pastors and invite them to join in. Without a doubt, the charismatic pastors have been far more interested than their evangelical counterparts. I have found the same to be true at Fellowship Church. Most of the people who have a heart to pray have been encouraged in their prayer ministry through the charismatic movement.

> The charismatic movement especially has strengthened the church's prayer life.

Obviously, many great men and women of prayer, such as Bill Bright, Kay Arthur, and Henry Blackaby, are not charismatics. But most of the writing and speaking done these days on prayer is by charismatic pastors and leaders. My mailbox is often filled with announcements on prayer conferences and workshops, most of which are hosted by charismatic churches. Charismatics are calling the church to pray.

Why is an emphasis on prayer so central to the charismatic movement? One reason is its supernatural worldview. The charismatic worldview is very open to God's miraculous intervention in daily events. Prayer is the means by which we invite those interventions. Charismatic theology expects God to act in the here and now, and that adds fuel to one's passion to pray. Prayers may be answered at this very moment. The person being prayed for may be healed, delivered from a demon, given a prayer language, or overcome with emotional or physical manifestations of the Spirit. This kind of expectancy creates a climate of faith that nurtures a believer's prayer life.

The belief in a prayer language—praying in an unknown language—also enhances prayer. John Sherrill devotes an entire chapter to the question, Why should anyone want to speak in tongues? He includes a sampling of testimonies from believers who have found their prayer language strengthening their prayer life:

"What's the use of speaking in tongues? The only way I can answer that is to say, 'What's the use of a bluebird? What is the use of a sunset? Just sheer, unmitigated bliss, just joy unspeakable and with it health and peace and rest and release from burdens and tension.'" Marianne Brown, housewife, Parkersburg, Pennsylvania. . . .

"I am built up, am given joy, courage, peace, the sense of God's presence; and I happen to be a weak person who needs this." William T. Sherwood, seventy-five-year-old Episcopal priest, St. Petersburg, Florida.[1]

Many have found a spiritual language adding richness and pleasure to their prayer life, thus making prayer a more enjoyable and desirable way to serve God.

Another reason why charismatic churches are often praying churches is that they believe that God calls some to a specific ministry of intercession. Intercessors are prayer warriors whose primary ministry is prayer. Some of these men and women give three-to-six hours to prayer daily. Prayer is not seen as something to do after they have done their ministry; prayer *is* their ministry. The charismatic movement has done a good job of identifying, mobilizing, and training these gifted intercessors.

The belief in spiritual warfare embraced by charismatic churches raises the primacy of prayer. Prayer becomes hand-to-hand combat with the enemy. Intercession becomes guerrilla warfare behind enemy lines, waged to set prisoners free. Prayer is a real weapon hurled at a real enemy with real power manifested in real demons influencing real people and places. Prayer is not theory, but a matter of life and death—a key to spiritual survival.

A final reason why the charismatic movement has become a hotbed for prayer is the belief that God talks back when you pray. Prayer is not seen as one-way communication, but as a dialogue in which the Father may respond to the prayer by speaking through an impression, dream, or prophetic word. Communication is always easier when both parties participate. Prayer is easier when you expect that God might answer your prayer right there, at the very moment you are praying.

What can the word and power church learn from the charismatic movement about prayer?

1. We need to give people a good hands-on, practical theology of prayer. Most teaching on prayer is guilt-based and vaguely motivational ("Martin Luther prayed three hours a day, and when he had a really tough day ahead, he prayed four!"), but too often our people don't understand how prayer actually works. Prayer for many is like flossing teeth: They do it because they know that if they don't, something really bad might happen. There's no real delight in it.

Evangelical writers have done a good job of laying a theological foundation for prayer. Andrew Murray's book *The Ministry of Intercession* is a classic example. The staff at Fellowship profited from reading this wonderful little book. Charismatic writers have taken the church's theology of prayer and are making it practical. God seems to even be raising up a "cottage industry" of writers and speakers who do nothing but write about prayer, speak about prayer, and pray. They provide practical training on issues like

How can I pray for healing?
What is the role of prayer in spiritual warfare?

What is the ministry of intercession?
What is the role of prayer in taking a city for Christ?
How can I pray for unreached people?
How can I pray for people in demonic oppression?
How can I learn to hear God's voice when I pray?
What is the place of spiritual language in my prayer life?

Some of the authors who have had the biggest impact on Fellowship Church regarding prayer are Peter Wagner, Cindy Jacobs, Dutch Sheets, Ted Haggard, John Dawson, Mike Bickle, and Ed Silvoso. God blesses the humble of heart. Part of my personal journey has been to admit that I don't have all the answers and to sit at the feet of those who know more than I do. We can do that by reading good books. We also can profit from attending many of the prayer conferences that are now held many times a year all across the country. These conferences combine good teaching, powerful testimonies of answered prayer, and a faith-drenched environment with hands-on opportunities to pray.

2. We need to identify and mobilize prayer intercessors. There are about forty intercessors at Fellowship Church; that is, people who identify their primary ministry as intercession. Four of these have left their full-time jobs and established ministries whereby they can intercede full time. The rest include mothers, high school students, and retirees. These people love to pray. They pray through each of our four Sunday services. They often pray through the night for our city. They prayer-walk our neighborhoods. They meet with me on Friday afternoons to pray for Sunday's services. They fast. They hear from the Lord. They pray for healing. They lead prayer cells. They teach others how to pray.

When God first began to raise up intercessors in our church, I was afraid of them. Their gifting is very different from my own. Even the way they talk about the spiritual life is different than how I express my faith. They often see life in abstract terms, while for me life is more concrete. They like to have quiet times in Ezekiel; I like Romans. They pray more fervently and longer than I do, which was intimidating at first. I think they had a hard time trusting me at first, too.

About four years ago we realized that if we were really going to celebrate the richness of both evangelical and charismatic traditions, we had to learn how to minister together. It would have been very easy for our intercessors to leave and settle into a charismatic church that appreciated them more, and it would have been easy for me to surround myself only with people who think and act like me. Sadly, this tendency reveals why our churches are often unbalanced. We tend to flock together and join with people who are just like us, losing the potential richness of a body that embraces its diversity in Christ.

We—the intercessors and I—have hung in there, bumped and bruised each other, and laughed and cried along the way, and today our intercession ministry is a source of immense spiritual power for Fellowship Church. We have learned how to listen to one another and respect our differences. We trust one another now. Tonight I am tired and lonely as I spend another season away from my family writing, wondering if I am ever going to finish this book that beckons my time and energy. But I am comforted to know that all my intercessors are praying for me, because I sent them my monthly prayer letter this week. I think they know that they are very important to me and to our church.

> We tend to flock together and join with people who are just like us, losing the potential richness of a body that embraces its diversity in Christ.

Pastors, identify your intercessors. Start praying with them once a week. Invite them into your leadership meetings, and ask them what they are hearing from the Lord. Attend a prayer conference with them. Be vulnerable with your needs and invite them to pray for you.

3. We need to free up pastors to make prayer a priority in their lives. I have noticed that the charismatic pastors in our city have greater freedom in their schedules to spend time in prayer. One of the greatest gifts my congregation has given me is the freedom to pray. Each Thursday I fast and pray and spend the day in an isolated cabin, seeking God in prayer for our church. Friday afternoons I pray with our intercessors. Saturday nights I pray with our worship team. The church staff gathers for prayer each Wednesday morning, and we try to spend a half-day in prayer once a month. Recently Fellowship allowed me to travel with one of our prayer teams to Vietnam just to pray. The church has allowed me to serve our city's prayer movement. Freeing me up to pray has been a sacrifice for the congregation, because I am not as accessible as I otherwise would be.

But they believe, as I do, that the pastor's greatest priority is to meet with God.

The first church elders said, "We will . . . give our attention to prayer and the ministry of the word" (Acts 6:3–4). Dare we devote ourselves to anything else?

Share stories of answered prayer. Pentecostalism, the spiritual parent of the charismatic movement, places the time of testimony at the heart of the church's corporate life. Could this be why there is so much faith in a prayer-answering God in these churches?

Several years ago a young mother in Fellowship named Beth lay in critical condition with spinal meningitis in the intensive care unit. I pulled the nurse aside, explained who I was, and asked her to let me know the odds. She gently said that there was little hope for this young mother. As I left the hospital, I passed by the dozens of friends and family who were praying in the waiting room—passed by them knowing what they didn't know. And I began to prepare Beth's funeral service.

I am glad Beth's friends didn't know what I knew. They were naïve enough to believe God could really heal her. They prayed for her through the night and through the next day, and one day led to two days and two to four—until her eyes opened and she was healed. I will never forget the Sunday Beth returned to church and shared with the congregation what God had done for her. Even today, I rejoice in God's power and goodness when I see Beth each Sunday.

4. We need to sensitively and appropriately create an openness to spiritual language in the congregation. No one can convince me that a believer must have a prayer language to have a rich prayer life. Many believers have great power in prayer without praying in a spiritual language. Yet some in the body of Christ (including me) find their spiritual language a great aid to prayer. I guess some of us need more help than others! Because this is a sensitive or unfamiliar matter to some, we will devote the next chapter to cultivating a healthy environment in which those who pray this way and those who do not can enjoy and not offend one another.

THE KINGDOM OF GOD IS HERE IN PART

We have already noted that Jesus' teaching about the kingdom of God can be confusing at times. Sometimes he says the kingdom of God is present today (Matt. 12:28). At other times he declares that the kingdom will not come until a future time (Matt. 8:11). Theologian George Eldon Ladd's work regarding this tension has helped many of us understand Christ's teaching on the kingdom. Two dog-eared copies of his book *The Gospel of the Kingdom* sit on my shelf. Ladd coined the phrase "already, but not yet" to describe the kingdom of God. He writes,

> The kingdom of God belongs to the Age to Come. Yet the Age to Come has overlapped with This Age. We may taste its powers and thereby be delivered from This Age and no longer live in conformity to it. This new transforming power is the power of the Age to Come; it is indeed the power of the Kingdom of God. The Kingdom of God is future, but it is not only future. Like the powers of The Age to Come, the Kingdom of God has invaded this evil Age that men may know something of its blessings even while the evil Age lives on.[2]

Signs and wonders are the sparks that fly when two kingdoms collide. Jesus said, "If I drive out demons by the Spirit of God, then the kingdom of God has come upon you" (Matt. 12:28). Jesus preached "the good news of the kingdom" and went about "healing every disease and sickness among the people" (Matt. 4:23). Healing and deliverance mark the coming of the kingdom.

Evangelicals are right to remind us that the kingdom of God is not fully here and that suffering is part of living in a fallen world. Charismatics are equally correct to remind the church that the kingdom of God is here in some ways, that eternity has broken into time in Christ, and that we might expect these breakthroughs to occur whenever God's people gather expectantly and ask him to heal.

Healing prayer needs to be a regular rhythm in the ministry cycle of a word and power church. James makes it clear that healing prayer is part of the elder's shepherding ministry over the flock: "Is any one of you sick? He should call the elders of the church to pray over him" (James 5:14). The prophet Ezekiel thundered this indictment against Israel's disobedient shepherds: "You have not strengthened the weak or healed the sick or bound up the injured" (Ezek. 34:4).

> Healing prayer needs to be a regular rhythm in the ministry cycle of a word and power church.

Word and power churches are healing churches where prayer for emotional and physical healing is a regular part of body life through small groups, ministry teams, and worship services.

At the time I graduated from seminary, my understanding of what it meant to shepherd a flock had no place for healing. I was trained to help people find meaning in suffering. The charismatic movement has brought balance to me in this area, reminding me that we serve a God who still heals today. Now we are trying to become a church where people both find meaning in suffering *and* are healed.

We are presently reorganizing the elder ministry so that our elders will be more available to pray for the flock. We are also exploring ways to increase our ability to pray for people after services and in small groups. We designed our new worship center with a large prayer room so people can be prayed for throughout and after each service as well as during the week.

Some of our richest times together have been evenings of prayer for specific needs. A mother in our congregation who struggled with infertility problems asked us several years ago to have a prayer service just for parents who were struggling with conceiving a child. We spent an evening in prayer, and about a fourth of those present now have little ones!

This past week I spoke with a man whose forty-year-old daughter has been diagnosed with Alzheimer's disease. He said his daughter and son-in-law recently left their church and found a new one. "Why?" I asked. "Because they wanted to go to a church with a healing service," he replied. Divine healing is this woman's only hope.

Shouldn't every church be able to offer hope to the sick—both the hope of finding meaning in suffering and the hope that God may, in his mercy, break into time and let the sparks of the kingdom fly in healing power? Healing ministries will look different in every congregation. The important application for the word and power church is to determine what this looks like for you.

GOD SPEAKS TODAY

Every Christian believes that God speaks. This is part of what it means to be a follower of Christ: to live in an abiding, conversational relationship with a God who loves us enough to communicate with us. Evangelicals remind us that the primary means by which God speaks to us is Scripture. Charismatics remind us that God speaks to us in other ways as well. Different traditions focus on different biblical texts. God raises up these traditions to "dust off" certain portions of Scripture and call the church to reexamine them. The charismatics have dusted off 1 Corinthians 12:4–11:

> There are different kinds of gifts, but the same Spirit. There are different kinds of service, but the same Lord. There are different kinds of working, but the same God works all of them in all men. Now to each one the manifestation of the Spirit is given for the common good. To one there is given through the Spirit the message of wisdom, to another the message of knowledge by means of the same Spirit, to another faith by the same Spirit, to another gifts of healing by that one Spirit, to another miraculous powers, to another prophecy, to another distinguishing between spirits, to another speaking in different kinds of tongues, and to still another the interpretation of tongues. All these are the work of one and the same Spirit, and he gives them to each one, just as he determines.

Paul was giving the Corinthians guidelines about how to worship together. Word had come to Paul that they were abusing some of the spiritual gifts, especially speaking in tongues. Paul was not writing to condemn any spiritual gift, but to instruct the church in how they are to be used properly.

This is not the only passage in the Bible about spiritual gifts. What is unique about this passage is that some of these gifts are revelatory gifts: The Holy Spirit subjectively reveals himself to us through them. The Bible uses the term *revelation* in several different ways. Sometimes the word *apokalypsis* refers to scriptural revelation, which is divinely authoritative. At other times the same word is used to describe a message with less authority; in such passages the word means "divinely prompted guidance or direction" (1 Cor. 14:26; Gal. 2:2; Eph. 1:17; Phil. 3:15). I am using the second meaning when I speak of revelatory gifts. Let's consider several of the revelatory gifts Paul mentions in 1 Corinthians 12:4–11.

The message of wisdom and the message of knowledge. What do these phrases mean? These are difficult words to define precisely, because this is the only time these phrases are mentioned in the Bible (in the King James Version, "word of wisdom" and "word of knowledge"). The Greek word for *word* or *message* is *logos*. These messages impart divinely revealed wisdom or knowledge in order to build others up. Paul calls these messages "manifestations of the Spirit"—they are spiritually revealed or disclosed. There is the hint of the supernatural about these messages; they have information or insight not naturally known by the speaker.

One evening after services we were praying for a woman with chronic back pain. We waited quietly to hear how the Spirit wanted us to pray. I received a gentle impression that God was not so interested in her back that night, but in her heart. Then I was prompted to ask her about an experience she had with her mother in junior high. She began to weep, and a deep emotional scar opened up as she recalled incidents in her seventh-grade year that had led her to make sinful choices, keeping her locked in anger. God began to set her free from that as we prayed, guided by the Spirit, for an emotional need instead of a physical one. I believe that I received a word of wisdom or knowledge from God to help me minister to our friend.

Jack, a leader in our church, was powerfully touched by a word of wisdom one evening in his small group. Jack is a godly, committed Christian leader but had always struggled with connecting emotionally with God and with others. Frustrated and broken, he began to fast and eventually called together some close friends for an evening of prayer for him. During the prayer, God gave a word to one of the group members that related to Jack's father. The Holy Spirit immediately touched Jack's heart and revealed a wound that had been festering for thirty years. Jack began to sob. The group held him as he wept. Today Jack is a different man. His love for others and his heart for God are greatly intensified. God used a word of wisdom to set him free.

Prophecy. A good definition of prophecy is "telling something that God has spontaneously brought to mind."[3] Paul highly prized this gift, exhorting the Corinthians to "eagerly desire spiritual gifts, especially the gift of prophecy" (1 Cor. 14:1).

Does Paul imagine a handful of Old Testament prophets, declaring God's Word with the authority of Scripture? No. The gift of prophecy, rather than being the possession of a select few, may be received by any New Testament Christian. Peter quoted Joel's prophecy in explaining the new age of the Spirit that was birthed at

Pentecost: "'I will pour out my Spirit in those days, and they will prophesy'" (Acts 2:18). What days are these? Peter clearly applied this prophecy to our time—the days we live in. Peter cites Joel to affirm that the church age, begun at Pentecost, will be marked by a spirit of prophecy poured out upon men and women.

It is important to notice the difference between Old Testament prophecy and New Testament prophecy. Old Testament prophets spoke with the authority of Scripture. *New Testament prophets do not.* In fact, Paul demands that prophecies be tested by other believers present (1 Cor. 14:29). Can you imagine anyone "testing" an Old Testament prophet like Jeremiah or Isaiah? But Paul goes as far as disobeying a prophecy (Acts 21:4–5)!

> It is important to notice the difference between Old Testament prophecy and New Testament prophecy.

Paul calls these words of prophecy *revelations.* "If a revelation comes to someone who is sitting down, the first speaker should stop" (1 Cor. 14:30). Paul is not using the term in the technical sense used by theologians when they refer to Scripture. He is using the word more broadly to mean "communication from God that does not result in written Scripture or words equal to written Scripture in authority."[4] Prophetic words are impressions or burdens from God that we share with others to build them up. They may speak of the future, but don't have to.

I am aware that some "prophetic words" seem to border on the bizarre and are often delivered in dramatic fashion. Some churches make the prophetic the center of their ministry. Our experience with prophetic ministry is not nearly so spectacular. The prophetic in our body is woven naturally into the simple rhythms of our corporate life.

Last week my wife and I hosted an end-of-the-year cookout for one of the ministry teams at Fellowship Church. We invited whole families and spent the evening dodging raindrops, flipping burgers, and making s'mores treats. We ended the evening by worshiping together as families. Toward the end of the worship time, I sensed God's presence drawing near and asked everyone to come and gather together on the floor: "Let's wait on God for a moment and see what he might say to us." We waited quietly for several minutes. "Is anyone hearing anything?" I asked the group. "I think I am," a mother of two replied. "I'm sensing that we are to encourage Jan by having the children pray for her. I think God wants to bless Jan through the kids tonight."

"That's what I'm sensing too," a man replied.

Jan is battling multiple sclerosis and had been sitting throughout the worship because her legs were numb. The children gathered around Jan, laid hands on her, and prayed gentle, simple prayers of blessing and healing. Jan wept as these little ones ministered to her in response to a prophetic word.

Tongues and the interpretation of tongues. A good general definition of speaking in tongues is "prayer or praise spoken in syllables not understood by the speaker."[5] We see the gift of tongues functioning in three different ways in the New Testament. Acts 2 shows that the gift of tongues can be the ability to proclaim the gospel in a language unknown to the speaker.

A second use of the gift of tongues is as a private devotional prayer language. The gift of tongues as practiced in Corinth served a different purpose than it served at Pentecost. Throughout 1 Corinthians 14, Paul contrasts public tongues speaking with another kind of tongues speaking that he practiced outside the church setting. "I thank God that I speak in tongues more than all of you. But in the church I would rather speak five intelligible words to instruct others than ten thousand words in a tongue" (1 Cor. 14:18–19).

What type of tongues speaking does Paul practice apart from church? The best explanation is that he is referring to a private prayer language. Paul describes this kind of praying as "speaking to God" (1 Cor. 14:2) and says a person "who speaks in a tongue edifies himself" (1 Cor. 14:4); he encourages people to use this gift privately (1 Cor. 14:5). I spent an evening in a theological library looking up every commentary I could find on this passage. I found that most scholars believe that Paul was describing a personal prayer language in 1 Corinthians 14 when he speaks of praying in tongues outside of church. Eugene Peterson's paraphrase of Scripture, *The Message*, reflects the most common interpretation:

> If you praise him in the private language of tongues, God understands you but no one else does, for you are sharing intimacies just between you and him. . . . The one who prays using a private "prayer language" certainly gets a lot out of it, but proclaiming God's truth to the church in its common language brings the whole church into growth and strength. (1 Cor. 14:1–4)

The third use of tongues is as a public message in tongues that is interpreted by one with the gift of interpretation. When this public tongues message is interpreted properly, it serves as a prophetic word for the assembly. Paul is adamant that there be no tongues speaking without interpretation: "If anyone speaks in a tongue, two—or at the most three—should speak, one at a time, and someone must interpret. If there is no interpreter, the speaker should keep quiet in the church and speak to himself and God" (1 Cor. 14:27–28).

One evening in Vietnam our prayer team gathered in our hotel for prayer. During the prayer time, one of the members prayed in tongues, and another interpreted. God seemed to be calling two people into a special, lifelong ministry to the Vietnamese. God used the message in tongues, along with many other factors, to clarify this couple's life mission.

No charismatic leader I know of believes that these revelatory gifts speak with the same authority as Scripture. Rather, these gifts are "divinely prompted guidance or direction" that needs to be tested and weighed against Scripture.

I am personally indebted to the charismatic movement for dusting off 1 Corinthians 12–14 and calling the church to embrace all of God's good gifts, including these. True, some fellowships have swung out of balance and seem to believe that these are the only important gifts. We must be wary of overemphasizing any gift in relation to the others.

> We must be wary of overemphasizing any gift in relation to the others.

These gifts have broadened my understanding of how people change, heal, and grow. I have always known that the Word changes people, that prayer changes people, that loving relationships change people. My charismatic brothers and sisters have taught me that revelatory words, spoken with humility and sensitivity, change people, too.

The primary purpose of the prophetic ministry in the New Testament is encouragement (1 Cor. 14:3). These gifts have a unique ability to express the tenderness and mercy of the Lord to hurting people. Some of the best times of ministry for me have come after a good evening in the Scriptures, worship, and prayer when needs are laid bare and the Spirit whispers gentle words of hope and promise. Typically, these are words that remind Christians who they are and how much they are loved.

The revelatory gifts also lead us to encounter the awesome presence of God. Paul tells us that when a prophetic word is given before "an unbeliever or someone who does not understand . . . , the secrets of his heart will be laid bare. So he will fall down and worship God, exclaiming, 'God is really among you!'" (1 Cor. 14:24–25). I have seen this happen with believers as well as unbelievers. When a body of believers comes together around the Word of God, prayer, and fellowship, and the revelatory gifts bring words that pierce the heart with their supernatural accuracy, everyone present knows God is in the place.

Paul links the revelatory gifts with gifts of healing. I am amazed at how gently and accurately the Spirit leads his people when we are ministering to someone in healing prayer. We are learning not just to pray, but to stop and ask the Spirit to show us what he wants us to pray for. He often will release his gifts and guide us into the broken places of the soul. Six of us gathered one night to pray for a successful young businessman who had fallen into depression. He was immobilized by fear and gripped with inadequacy. We spent six hours with him that night, gently asking the Spirit to reveal areas of brokenness and sin in his heart. God answered—with alarming specificity, leading us to people, places, and events that no one in the group knew other than the businessman, events he himself had not thought of in years. Our brother found freedom that night.

I have found the revelatory gifts a great encouragement to my study of the Scriptures. Each Friday I pray with a group of intercessors about Sunday's sermon. God often speaks specific words through the intercessors that help me understand what he wants to do Sunday morning. These words don't become the sermon; they help me apply the sermon.

Several times, words like these spoken over me have given me great comfort and encouragement to press on. The Bible always comforts me, but when the Lord has a word for a specific need I am facing, I feel even closer to my Shepherd. Paul encouraged young Timothy, "Do not neglect your gift, which was given you through a prophetic message when the body of elders laid their hands on you" (1 Tim. 4:14.) Paul's timid disciple found encouragement when he remembered the elders' prophetic words. We can find that, too.

It bothers me when people question my commitment to the Scriptures because I believe in the revelatory gifts. I would *die* for the Scriptures. I preach them faithfully and believe they are central to the spiritual life. I spent many years in seminary to learn them better. Why must the revelatory gifts be seen as opposing the study of Scripture? I find that the revelatory gifts are most often given in an environment where Scripture has been faithfully taught. These gifts often bring Scripture to bear directly on a person's life need. They are not the Bible's foe, but its friend.

> The revelatory gifts are most often given in an environment where Scripture has been faithfully taught.

A positive concept emerging from American churches since the church growth movement began is gift-based ministry. The premise is simple: Every believer has a spiritual gift. Believers are most effective and fruitful when they are ministering according to their unique gifting. Churches that are mobilizing their people well are helping them discover their spiritual gifts and giving them specific training and opportunities to use them.

Usually the training focuses on the ministry gifts found in passages like Romans 12:4–8 and 1 Peter 4:10–11, the latter reading, "Each one should use whatever gift he has received to serve others" (v. 10). The "service gifts" mentioned in these passages are different from the revelatory gifts Paul lists in 1 Corinthians 12:7–11. Some of the gifts mentioned include teaching, serving, leading, giving, and helping. These gifts appear to be given to the believer at conversion. We can devote the rest of our lives to sharpening our ability to exercise our spiritual gifts.

Revelatory gifts are different in that they are manifestations of the Spirit, given in the moment, and not gifts intrinsic to who we are. Yet these gifts call for training, too. Word and power churches need to train their people in understanding how and when and where to minister in these gifts. It is unwise to have a ministry focused solely on the revelatory gifts. It is also unwise to have a ministry focused solely on the service gifts. Healthy churches train their people to minister in both types of gifts.

WORSHIP IS PARTICIPATORY

The most obvious way the charismatic movement has impacted the church today is through worship. Charismatic worship is so pervasive today that hardly any portion of the body of Christ remains untouched. Here again, we face the "genius of the AND." Evangelicalism has brought us the rich doctrinal hymns that have sustained us for centuries. Charismatic worship need not replace the classic hymns of the faith, but complement them; it serves to meet needs in the worshiper that the classic hymns do not.

Charismatic worship was born on the beaches of Southern California during the Jesus People movement of the sixties. Chuck Smith preached the gospel to the young people on the beaches and gathered them into a new church he called Calvary Chapel, which soon began to express itself with worship songs that reflected his generation's hunger for intimacy with God. In the late seventies, a converted rock-and-roll singer named John Wimber poured passion into the simple lyrics of the Jesus People and developed a theology of worship that called people into an encounter with God. He had left a strong evangelical church "with a full head and an empty heart" and set out to birth a church that could rekindle a passion for Jesus. Worship was to become the hallmark of the Vineyard movement, which Wimber founded.

Evangelical hymns help the believer consider the majestic otherness of God. Their lyrics are doctrinally meaty, historic, and profound, requiring a lot of attention to the text as well as to the music. The great hymns focus on God's transcendence. Charismatic praise songs help the believer encounter the closeness of God. Their lyrics are more simple, personal, and intimate. These songs call the worshiper to experience God's immanence.

Charismatic worship begins with Hebrews 10:19–22 as its theological cornerstone:

> Therefore, brothers, since we have confidence to enter the Most Holy Place by the blood of Jesus, by a new and living way opened for us through the curtain, that is, his body, and since we have a great priest over the house of God, let us draw near to God with a sincere heart in full assurance of faith.

Charismatic worship enables us to *draw near* to God's presence. Wimber described the worship event as a relational process with several stages, each of which draws the believer closer to the Father's heart. Consider the analogy of a husband and wife preparing for intimacy. They do not immediately rush into the bedroom; they take time to draw close to one another. One meaning of the Greek word for worship, *proskuneo,* is "to turn toward to kiss." Psalm 2:12 calls us to "kiss the Son, lest he be angry." A flowing pattern of worship, with smooth transitions between a number of songs uninterrupted by announcements and solos, prepares us to "kiss," to express our most tender affection to, our Lord.

Wimber developed a five-phase model describing the flow of charismatic worship. The *invitation* phase is a call to worship. The opening song draws people into worship. The lyric is directed toward the people, not to God, and tells them what they are about to do. The *engagement* phase is similar to an engagement period before marriage. The lyric is now addressed to the Lord, not to one another. The third phase is *exaltation,* in which people sing out to the Lord, focusing on his majesty and greatness. Lyrics include words like *great, majestic, worthy, reigns, Lord,* and *mountains.* The people spend a brief time singing to God. In the *adoration* phase, the people are seated, and the songs now allow the people to sing to God. The key words may be *Jesus* and *you.* The last phase is the *intimacy* phase. This is the quietest and most tender time in the worship session. We address God as *Abba* or *Daddy* in this phase. Here the worshiper is now present with the Father in the Holy of Holies and is prepared to receive the Word.[6]

> Charismatic worship has also recaptured a historic Jewish element of worship: expressiveness.

Charismatic worship invites everyone into the worship process. The congregation is the choir. Each individual member, whether gifted musically or not, is invited to praise God. This is made easier by the contemporary style of the worship songs. Whether we like to admit it or not, most of us are not trained to appreciate nineteenth-century classical music. Most Americans like the music they grew up with, and for the boomer generations and those who follow, that music is rock and roll. Martin Luther took the tunes of the great drinking songs of the day and turned them into hymns. The charismatic movement has followed suit, taking advantage of the boomer generation's love for rock and roll and using it as a way to praise God.

Charismatic worship has also recaptured a historic Jewish element of worship: expressiveness. A quick read of the psalms finds a worshiping people who danced, bowed, leaped, waved banners, and raised their hands before God. Today these same expressions of worship are being restored to the church, thanks to the charismatic movement.

Word and power churches draw heavily on charismatic worship styles, mingling them with their own unique patterns of worship. What, practically, does this mean?

1. Word and power churches give careful consideration to their worship format. Certainly there is a variety of ways to invite worshipers into God's presence—Wimber's fivefold phase approach is not the only way. But it is a good way and is being adopted by many of America's growing churches. Does your worship format lead people into the presence of God?

2. Each church determines the appropriate balance between hymns and choruses. Many younger people like me simply have a hard time worshiping to the classic hymns, although we enjoy their doctrinal content. This is even more true with the generation behind the boomers. Balanced worship leads the believer into both the transcendence and the immanence of God. Does yours do both?

Congregations who find that the hymns are not connecting with the next generation but don't want to lose the rich doctrine found in them should not lose hope. There is a growing tendency to take the great hymns and rearrange them in a contemporary style. The Promise Keepers, working with Maranatha Music, have done an excellent job at this. There is also an encouraging trend toward writing more praise songs with richer doctrinal content.

3. Word and power churches create a worship environment where there is freedom to worship the Lord in either expressive or nonexpressive ways. Some people worship with raised hands and closed eyes, standing up in a stirring song. Others worship more reservedly. Healthy congregations create the freedom to do both.

4. Word and power churches embrace the arts. Dance, drama, and banners are just a few of the ways that worship can be enhanced. The arts will be especially helpful to the younger generation, which is much more image-oriented than the generations preceding it.

THE SPIRIT'S CHARISMATIC GIFTS CAN BE BEST EXPERIENCED IN THE CONTEXT OF RELATIONSHIPS

Small groups provide an excellent training ground for exploring the treasures brought to us by the charismatic movement. Paul describes how these gifts functioned in the Church at Corinth in 1 Corinthians 14:26: "When you come together, everyone has a hymn, or a word of instruction, a revelation, a tongue or an interpretation."

New Testament scholar Wayne Meeks tells us, "The meeting places of the Pauline groups, and probably of most other early Christian groups, were private houses." The house church was "the basic cell of the Christian movement." The only passage we have describing a New Testament church practicing the charismatic gifts, then, describes a small group of believers ministering to one another and the Lord in one of their homes.

That doesn't mean there is no place for these gifts in the larger worship service. Each congregation needs to determine for itself what is appropriate in the larger setting. It is interesting to observe,

> Small groups provide an excellent training ground for exploring the treasures brought to us by the charismatic movement.

though, that many Pentecostal and charismatic churches have backed away from practicing the charismatic gifts in the corporate worship service and have moved this ministry into their small groups instead. This makes good sense.

A small group is a safe place to make mistakes. If someone errs in mishandling a prophetic word, for example, a few are impacted, not an entire congregation. It's also easier to give and receive feedback in a small group. Moreover, it's required by Scripture. Paul teaches that "the spirits of prophets are subject to the control of prophets" (1 Cor. 14:32). This assumes an environment where people are in community together. They know each other well enough to say, "That doesn't sound right to me," or to have questions about the character of the one ministering.

Small groups are also highly conducive to healing prayer. Good groups are built on the foundation of trusting relationships. They are safe places where deep needs are shared and enduring friendships are built. What better place to learn how to pray for healing?

Small groups are living organisms. They grow and mature. A good small group needs to grow in its ability to minister the Word. A good small group also needs to grow in its ability to practice the charismatic gifts. The first experience with the gifts in a group can feel clumsy and nonproductive. Groups that keep practicing, though, eventually learn to work together like a fine symphony. Group members learn to trust one another, listen to the Spirit's prompting, and discern when to speak and when to remain silent. The community collectively learns how to yield to the Spirit's agenda and join with him where he is at work. Just as each musician in a symphony plays a critical role in the performances of the concert, God uses each group member to contribute to what he wants to do in the evening.

Jesus chose a small group to live with while on earth. It makes sense that he would choose a small group to be a special place of visitation among his people.

↩

Word and power churches draw together the best of both evangelical and charismatic traditions. Are you ready for a checklist? How would you rate your church on each of the ten topics we have considered?

1. Expository preaching
2. An emphasis on the authority of Scripture
3. A realistic affirmation that the kingdom of God is not yet fully here
4. A belief that spiritual growth is a process
5. A belief that the Word can best be studied and applied in the context of relationships
6. An emphasis on prayer
7. A hopeful affirmation that the kingdom is here in part
8. A belief that God speaks today
9. An emphasis on participatory worship
10. A belief that the Spirit's charismatic gifts can be best experienced in the context of relationships

WHERE DO WE GO FROM HERE?

Whenever two rivers flow into one, there is turbulence. Merging the mighty waters of the evangelical and charismatic traditions is not easy, but it can be done. And it *must* be done if we are going to meet the challenge of the hour. God is raising up thousands of churches that are tired of living under the "tyranny of the OR" and want all God has for them. What does a word and power church look like? The following chapters attempt to answer that question.

STUDY QUESTIONS

1. "Nothing ruins a good stereotype better than actually meeting the person you have been caricaturing." Have any of your stereotypes been "ruined"?

2. Discuss the strengths of the charismatic church:
   A. Prayer is essential
   B. The kingdom of God is here in part
   C. God speaks today
   D. Worship is participatory
   E. The Spirit's charismatic gifts can be best experienced in the context of relationships

3. In which areas does your church excel? How can your church grow in the areas in which it is weak?

PART TWO
Inside the Word and Power Church

Chapter Seven
IN THE PRESENCE OF A TALKING GOD

Busy and Bewildered at Biola

Have you ever heard pastors joke about the years they spent in seminary when they argued with friends late into the evening about the subtleties of one theological position over another and solved the great questions of life over Diet Cokes and pizza?

My seminary experience wasn't like that. For starters, I was married. Sandi wasn't up for batting around supralapsarianism after a full day's work, and neither was I. I was also busy teaching English to freshmen at Biola University, pastoring at a local church, and preaching on the weekends at a little church just outside Palm Springs, California. And then there were the classes. I wanted to graduate in three years, so I took full course loads all the way through. That didn't leave much time for theological bantering with my buddies.

The downside of doing seminary the way I did it is that it didn't leave much time for the luxury of personal reflection or long walks with tweed-jacketed professors down ivy-covered pathways such as you see C. S. Lewis doing in the film *Shadowlands*. When you are confused about something, you learn the material, tuck your questions away somewhere, and figure you will tackle them later. I left seminary with a lot of questions, a lot of puzzle pieces that didn't quite fit together for me.

One of those questions dealt with how God speaks.

I hit seminary on the heels of the charismatic renewal of the seventies, which was marked by a wide-open willingness to "hear from

God" in every way imaginable. Certain "horror stories" swept our conservative campus, chronicling the abuses of those who claimed to hear from God. A man on a charismatic talk show said he had been swept into heaven in a vision and, for just $9.95, he would sell you his book and tell you what heaven looks like. Another story reported that a young man fell in love with a pretty young lady in his church who didn't return the favor. "The Lord has told me you are to marry me," he said. "Funny," she replied. "I wonder why he didn't tell me, too."

Some of the stories were not so funny. Jim Jones, a false prophet who claimed to speak from God, had just murdered several hundred of his followers in a South American jungle by inducing them to drink poisoned Kool-Aid. Jones thereby became Exhibit A in the defense's case against God's speaking today in ways other than the Bible.

The church suddenly seemed awash in dreams, visions, visits from angels, and "Thus saith the Lord" prophecies. My seminary professors were aghast as they watched a large portion of the body of Christ slide into the quicksand of subjectivism.

> Almost everyone I knew on our campus lived on a daily level with a God who speaks in ways other than the Bible.

Not surprisingly, a major theme during my time in seminary was a firm teaching on the authority of the Scripture and cracking down on "subjective mysticism." We learned that the canon is closed and that to suggest that God speaks in any other way compromises the Scriptures' authority and places us on the slippery slope of subjectivity.

The message was clear: God speaks through the Bible and the Bible only. Don't trust anything else.

There was just one problem. We didn't live that way. Almost everyone I knew on our campus lived on a daily level with a God who speaks in ways other than the Bible.

We called these communications from God "leadings" or "promptings" or "impressions" or "a still, small voice" (see 1 Kings 19:12 KJV). And we acted on these words from God.

Chapel speakers spoke about being roused in the night to pray for a fellow missionary.

We prayed for each other and sometimes were "prompted" to share something God had "put on our heart" for a friend.

Our professors, at times, changed their lesson plans, sensing that "God has something different for us today."

We used different terms from our charismatic cousins to describe God's speaking, and we were quite a bit more subdued about it (no one I knew got swept into heaven for a tour), but it slowly dawned on me that we basically believed the same thing. God speaks—and not just through his Word.

A Matter of Semantics

I have been out of seminary twelve years now, and while I still don't have much time for late-night theological chat sessions with buddies, I have wrestled with this question of hearing from God because it lies at the center of the spiritual life. One of my primary duties as a pastor is to help people learn how to hear from God. Do I teach them how to hear from God the evangelical way or the charismatic way? The answer is yes. I do both. I am convinced that when you pare away the externals that distract us, charismatics and evangelicals are basically saying the same thing about how God speaks.

What follows are two extended quotes from major Christian leaders. The first statement, from a sermon on prayer, is from Bruce Wilkinson, who has a degree from Dallas Seminary and is president of Walk Through the Bible ministries. He is preaching on prayer.

> On my first trip to Israel I was on a ship that docked on the Isle of Patmos, where John wrote Revelation. I was so lonely for my family I didn't even go back up to the cave where he wrote it. I wanted to be by myself so I walked the streets of Patmos until I found a coffee shop. I sat down and prayed, "Lord, I'm in the middle of nowhere. I don't know anyone. Send someone who needs You."
>
> The guy at the next table said, "Do you want some coffee? I'll buy. Are you off that ship?"
>
> "Yes," I said. I moved over to his table and he bought me a cup of coffee.
>
> I said, "What's the matter?"
>
> He said, "What do you mean what's the matter?"
>
> I said, "I don't know. What's the matter?"
>
> "I just left my wife and I'm not going back. I'm going to try to go on the ship to get to the next island so I can fly out of here."

"Would you believe I'm all the way from Atlanta, Georgia, for one reason—to get you back to your wife?"

"Impossible," he said.

"Let me return the favor of the coffee," I said. And for the next hour God broke through and that young man came to know Christ. I told him, "If you make it up with your wife before the boat leaves, you come wave."

"It'll never happen."

"You're a miracle. Give God a chance."

I got on the boat, and was praying like crazy. I went to the back of the boat overlooking the back of the harbor and will never forget what I saw. Down off the rocky cliff on this side of the boat comes this young couple, holding hands and waving!

I'm convinced that if I hadn't prayed, that man would have never said a word to me.[1]

The next quote is from the late John Wimber, founder of the Vineyard movement. His writings and ministry have encouraged the use of "words of wisdom" and "words of knowledge" in healing and evangelism. This story relates an encounter between Wimber and a man named Francisco.

I prayed, asking God what was going on in Francisco's life. He answered by giving me an impression in my mind: "That's my Spirit on him, and I am calling him to salvation." . . .

During the next class period, I continued praying for Francisco. About halfway into the hour, I sensed the Spirit of God again speaking to my heart: "It's going to be all right. Relax." I suddenly had a peace that God would answer my prayers for Francisco.

After the class ended, everyone left the classroom except Francisco and me. As I walked toward him, his head fell into his arms and he began weeping. . . . I took a deep breath and said, "I think God sent me, and he wants you to come to him."

Francisco stared at me for a moment, then began telling me why he could not turn to God. "I cannot live the life. I'm not good enough." He went on like that for thirty-five minutes. He had hardened his heart to the gospel. I had no idea what to say. As he continued talking, I became desperate for words. Then a strange thought came. "Francisco," I said, "do you know what a midwife is?"

"Yes," he answered.

"Do you know what a breech birth is?"

"Yes."

"That's what is wrong with you. You're breech. I'm trying to get you turned around so you can get born again."

"Do whatever you have to do," was his emphatic response. For some reason, his attitude instantly changed. Instead of fighting my words, he listened. When we finally prayed together, he went on for over forty minutes with one of the most eloquent prayers of faith I have ever heard.

After praying and crying and crying he asked, "How did you know?"

"Know what?"

"How did you know I was a male nurse?"

I did not know that. He had been an army nurse for twenty years. During that time he delivered hundreds of babies, many of them breech. When I likened his condition to that of a breech baby's, he knew God was speaking to him.[2]

Wimber and Wilkinson both believe in a God who speaks personally, directly, and lovingly into their lives. And I bet you do, too. This is normal spirituality, and it doesn't compromise one's firm commitment to the authority of Scripture.

Dallas Willard, an ordained Southern Baptist and professor of philosophy at the University of Southern California, reminds us, "The Spirit that inhabits us is not dumb. . . . It is simply beyond belief that two persons, so intimately related . . . would not speak to each other. How can there be personal relationships, a personal walk with God . . . without individualized communication?"[3]

The Scriptures compel us to embrace the "genius of the AND," whether we want to or not. Two truths are held in tension throughout Scripture:

- God's Word is authoritative. It is the final word. The canon is closed. There is no new authoritative revelation being given today.
- God speaks today through ways other than the Bible. The prophetic ministry is alive and well today.

THE AUTHORITY OF SCRIPTURE

"Scripture defines the center of gravity for evangelicalism," writes Oxford scholar Alister McGrath. "Scripture is, for evangelicals, the central legitimating resource of Christian faith and theology, the clearest window through which the face of Christ may be seen."[4] Charismatics believe this, too.

Scripture claims this authority for itself. "All Scripture is God-breathed and is useful for teaching, rebuking, correcting and training in righteousness" (2 Tim. 3:16). The Old Testament prophets begin their words hundreds of times with the introductory phrase, "Thus says the LORD." Jesus himself, citing Scripture, tells the devil, "Man does not live on bread alone, but on every word that comes from the mouth of God" (Matt. 4:4). Jesus sees the Scriptures as words from the very mouth of God.

The New Testament sees itself as equally authoritative with the Old Testament. Peter can call Paul's writings Scripture (2 Peter 3:15–16). Paul himself says his words are "the Lord's command" (1 Cor. 14:37).

"The authority of Scripture," writes theologian Wayne Grudem, "means that all the words in Scripture are God's words in such a way that to disbelieve or disobey any word in Scripture is to disobey God."[5]

Word and power churches are churches of the Word. We live by the Word and die by the Word. What the Word says, we do. We preach from the Word. We study the Word. We carry out church discipline by the Word. We raise our children in the Word, and we send them to far away lands as missionaries because of the Word. We face our fears and share our faith because of the Word. When storms come, we crawl under the Word for shelter. We give because of the Word. We stay married because of the Word. We avoid sexual immorality because of the Word.

We do this because the Word is a window into the One who is *the* Word, Jesus Christ. We meet his authority in his Word. And we bow to it there.

PROPHECY

Care to take a guess regarding what some of the Scripture's most frequently disobeyed commands are? Here is one of my top contenders: "Do not treat prophecies with contempt" (1 Thess. 5:20).

One of the ironies of the evangelical tradition is that we will die for the authority of Scripture while we simultaneously revolt against that authority when it comes to the prophetic gifts. Yet, in the same way that God's Word firmly declares its authority, it firmly calls us to embrace a prophetic ministry in our churches today.

What comes to mind when you hear the words *prophetic ministry?* For some, *weird* is the first word that pops up. Ten years ago, phrases like *prophetic ministry* reminded me of a matted-haired, middle-aged guy carrying a big Bible and having a wooden cross dangling around his neck and wandering from church to church in a Volkswagen van with Bible verses spray-painted on it, ruining worship services by thundering Old Testament–sounding threats of judgment when it got quiet enough for him to speak.

> One of the ironies of the evangelical tradition is that we will die for the authority of Scripture while we revolt against the prophetic gifts.

That's not what I think of anymore. I have come to see the prophetic ministry as one of God's good gifts to his people. It is not weird. It is beautiful.

If you were to take a piece of paper, write at the top "What God's Word says about the gift of prophecy," and open your Bible to 1 Corinthians 14, here is a sample of what you might write:

"Eagerly desire . . . the gift of prophecy" (1 Cor. 14:1)
"Everyone who prophesies speaks to men for their
    strengthening, encouragement and comfort" (v. 3)
"He who prophesies edifies the church" (v. 4)
"Be eager to prophesy" (v. 39)

Paul devotes more inspired Scripture to discussing the prophetic gift than he does any other spiritual gift. We are to eagerly desire this gift so that we can use it to build up the church.

What is the gift of prophecy? Recall from the last chapter Dr. Grudem's definition of prophecy: "telling something that God has spontaneously brought to mind." Prophetic ministry is simply another way of describing what it means to be in an intimate relationship with a talking God. Dallas Willard captures this reality in the title of one of his books: *In Search of Guidance: Developing a Conversational Relationship with God*.

Wouldn't one aspect of a conversational relationship with God be a growing ability to hear him speak? Wouldn't two friends want to talk? And wouldn't they want to do so personally, dynamically, and intimately? I asked one friend what he thinks of when he hears the phrase "prophetic ministry."

"God speaks," he said. "I think of hearing God's voice."

Being a Christian is living in a relationship with a speaking God.

PROPHETIC WORDS AND MINISTRY

In some corners of the kingdom, prophetic ministry comes from the speaking platform, where a person with the gift of prophecy gives words to the group. I have no doubt that God does minister this way. Yet our experience at Fellowship has been somewhat different. Usually the prophetic ministry takes place in small groups or "'ministry times" when we are praying for one another. God usually gives the prophetic word as a key to unlocking the secrets of the heart. Ministry prayer times often "break open" after a prophetic word.

Recently I spoke at a pastors' conference on spiritual passion. I brought my intercessory team with me. During the session we paused and said, "If you find yourselves robbed of spiritual passion, take a moment to stand right now and let your brothers and sisters pray for you."

A member of our prayer team and I prayed for one pastor.

"Rejection," my prayer partner said gently to the pastor. "I'm hearing the word 'rejection' and I want to tell you that the Lord has not rejected you." The pastor began to weep. After the seminar was over, he approached me and asked, "Who was that guy? I want him to pray for me some more." They found each other and disappeared into a hotel room for the afternoon. The pastor was grappling with a lifelong battle with feeling rejected by his family, his friends, and ultimately God. He pastored a small church and felt as if God was punishing him because it wasn't growing.

"How did you know I struggled with rejection?" he asked my friend.

"It's just God," my friend answered. God used a prophetic word to encourage a brother.

～⌐

One of the Fellowship leaders was at a singles' retreat. He was sitting next to a woman during a social activity when he sensed the Lord speaking: "She's in trouble. Suicide."

The leader tapped her on the shoulder and said, "Are you struggling? Perhaps with some difficult thoughts, like suicide?"

The woman confided that she had fought suicidal thoughts for a year and that the only reason she had not taken her life was because of her children. God used a prophetic word to reveal her needs and lead her to experience healing prayer.

⟿

A distinguished middle-aged gentleman came forward for prayer after a service. The service had ended with a dance about an estranged relationship between a mother and a daughter. "That dance was my story," he said. He then told of a painful rift between his wife and their daughter. The ministry team began to pray about this until one of the men praying said, "God has put on my heart the phrase 'man for the nation.'"

The man receiving prayer began to weep. He was about to take over a major evangelical movement in a foreign country and was wrestling with his call. Then God gently comforted him through a prophetic word, reminding him that he was indeed a man for that nation.

⟿

Prophetic ministry has often been a breath of Spirit-life in Fellowship Church. Rather than detracting from the Word, Spirit-inspired prophecy glorifies the Word by revealing the places where the balm of Scripture needs to be rubbed in.

BUT ISN'T THIS DANGEROUS?

Some people are concerned that engaging in prophetic ministries is spiritually "dangerous." Ken Gire addresses this reasonable fear:

> It could be argued . . . that to open the possibility of God's speaking through other means than the clear teaching of Scripture is to let in all sorts of confusion. After all, a window lets in pollen along with the breeze, flies along with the sunshine, the cackle of crows along with the cooing of doves.
>
> If that were your argument, I would have to agree.

But if we want fresh air, we have to be willing to live with a few flies.

Of course, we can shut out the flies and the pollen and the cackle of crows. And if a clean and quiet house is what's most important to us, perhaps that is what we should do. But if we do, we also shut out so much of the warmth, so much of the fragrance, so many of the sweet songs that may be calling us.[6]

I suspect most of us would prefer risking a few flies over enduring the stale air that comes from a closed house.

Metaphors are one thing. Real life is another. How do we create a church where the Word is revered and the prophetic ministry is encouraged without harming one another or falling into the swamp of mysticism?

We dare not underestimate the danger. The trail of church history is littered with the wreckage of movements and churches that unpinned themselves from their moorings of the Word and were swept away by the winds of fancy. We Christians are always seeking shortcuts—looking for an easy way to hear from God. It's seductively tempting to lay aside the sweaty spiritual disciplines of Bible study and Scripture meditation for the more exciting "prophetic word."

> Healthy churches revere the authority of Scripture while encouraging the prophetic ministry.

The truth is, we can have it both ways. Healthy churches revere the authority of Scripture while encouraging the prophetic ministry. Here are some practical steps churches can take as they attempt to live in the tension Scripture calls us to with regard to these matters.

1. Stress that Scripture and not prophetic utterances are the primary means of spiritual growth and guidance. Churches that de-emphasize the study and preaching of Scripture in favor of the dramatic prophetic gifts soon become out of balance, weak, and sensational. Prophetic gifts are valuable; however, because they are always tainted by the humanity of the messenger, they should not be the first place a Christian turns to for growth and guidance. Our greatest interest should be in Scripture, God's primary tool for building up the people of God. Only God's words recorded in *the* Word are purely inspired.

If I had to choose between a small group where there is nothing but Scripture study and a small group where there is nothing but sharing prophetic words, my choice would be the Scripture study every time. Fortunately, we don't have to choose between Scripture and prophecy. A healthy church, always making Scripture central, embraces both.

2. Learn how to hear the voice of God through the Scriptures. Sometimes a false dichotomy is made between how God speaks through prophecy and how God speaks through his Word. The subtle implication is, "Yes, God speaks through the Bible. But if you want a personal word, you need to have a prophetic word spoken to you." This view leaves the impression that the Bible is nothing more than a rule book, a dead letter, a list of principles that we need to read, while the real communication goes on through the more dramatic prophetic events.

> The Bible is not merely a list of principles. . . . We should expect divine encounters whenever we pick up the Word.

This is a terrible misunderstanding of the Word of God and its role in the believer's life. God speaks *through the Word of God!*

The Word is a living word. "We read Scripture in order to listen again to the word of God spoken, and when we do, we hear him speak. Somehow or other these words live."[7]

It has been interesting to watch the people of Fellowship grow in the prophetic ministry. At the same time, God has given them greater insight into his Word and a greater ability to hear his voice while immersed in Scripture. The unleashing of a prophetic ministry should draw a church into the Word. Indeed, there should be the excitement of prophetic encounter every time we open the Word.

Prophetic ministry *is* exciting. When God, through a friend, speaks a word drenched with the divine into the hidden corners of our hearts . . . wow! But the same kind of exciting encounter can happen in the Scriptures.

The Bible is not merely a list of principles. It is living and dynamic, containing the very breath of God's Spirit. We should expect divine encounters whenever we pick up the Word. We should hunger for more than good ideas or helpful stories from our time in the Scriptures. We should crave a touch from heaven, a direct word spoken by the breath of the Spirit into the very recesses of our hearts. God longs to have a conversational relationship with us, and his favorite way of carrying on that conversation is through the Scriptures.

Twentieth-century Christians have been influenced more than we would like to admit by the Enlightenment, the worldview that spawned the modern era with its optimistic belief in human reason and a distrust of the supernatural. Our boredom with the Bible can be traced, in part, to this influence. "The Enlightenment forced evangelicalism into adopting approaches to spirituality that have resulted in rather cool, detached, and rational approaches to Scripture, such as those that have been associated with the traditional 'Quiet Time.'"[8]

The time has come for a prophetic approach to Scripture that anticipates a divine encounter with a speaking God whenever we lay ourselves open before his Word.

3. Provide teaching on the prophetic gift as a regular part of church training and preaching. Given the amount of attention paid to this gift in Paul's writings, it is remarkable that so little teaching is offered on prophecy today. Word and power churches need solid doctrinal foundations. We need to preach and teach on the authority of Scripture. Yet we also must preach and teach on the vital ministry of the prophetic gifts. Failing to offer teaching on this subject is a failure to present the full counsel of God to the people. Word and power churches will find Grudem's *Systematic Theology* a helpful resource. Grudem attempts to do in theology what we are trying to do in the church: bring the best of the evangelical and charismatic traditions together.

Teaching on the gift must first explain what the gift is and then give careful attention to how the gift should be used in the local church. Teachers looking for material need not look much farther than 1 Corinthians 14. Congregations must "carefully weigh" prophecies. Here are four questions to ask when testing a prophecy.

a. Does the prophecy edify those who hear it? Some who are drawn to prophetic ministry take their cue from the Old Testament prophets. They typically bring only scathing words of wrath and judgment. This is a serious mistake. It is important to stress again that there is a tremendous difference between Old Testament prophecy and New Testament prophecy. In addition to a difference in authority, there is a difference in message. New Testament prophecy is primarily for "strengthening, encouragement and comfort" (1 Cor. 14:3). Spirit-inspired prophecies will build up the person hearing them.

Some time ago, I saw a friend at a conference. He said to me, "Boy, I really sense the Lord wants me to tell you that you are going to face a great physical trial in the days ahead. I don't know what it is, but I'll pray." Looking back, I have serious doubts whether that was truly a prophetic word. It gave me little encouragement and created an opportunity for fear. And it never came true.

b. *Does the prophecy agree with Scripture?* Spirit-led prophecy will always agree with Scripture because the Spirit of prophecy is the Spirit of Scripture. Many of the prophetic words I have heard are actually citations of Scripture applied to a specific situation. When the prophetic word does not speak a scriptural truth, the message in the word must be in perfect harmony with scriptural revelation.

This does not mean that prophecy cannot address certain specific events or details in a person's life that are not recorded in Scripture. It does mean that any behavioral change suggested by the specific prophetic word must match Scripture.

c. *Do others agree that the prophecy is of God?* Sometimes at the end of a Fellowship worship service, someone will sense that he or she has been given a prophetic word. We ask the person to share the word with an elder, who prays about it and then chooses whether or not the prophecy would be appropriate to share with the entire group.

When people share a word in the small group, they typically will ask, "Does this seem like something the Lord would say?" Words that don't find favor with the group are gently set aside.

d. *Does the person with the prophecy present it humbly?* Prophetic words should not be prefaced with the statement, "Thus says the Lord." This implies that the speaker believes he or she is ministering with inspired, inerrant authority and that the message is in fact a new portion of Holy Scripture. As we have seen, New Testament prophecy does not bear that kind of weight.

Scripture is *never* tainted by the humanness of the biblical author. Prophetic words *always* are, and they should be delivered with humility.

Applying these four tests to prophetic words will go a long way toward protecting a congregation from error and toward creating an environment that both honors Scripture and welcomes the prophetic.

4. Develop a longing in your church for hearing the voice of God. We serve a God who, to borrow a phrase from Francis Schaeffer, is both there and not silent. God speaks! What could possibly be more important than learning to listen to him?

The story of Scripture is the story of men and women who heard the voice of God and obeyed. He spoke to Adam. He spoke to Moses. He spoke to Isaiah. He spoke to Nehemiah. He spoke to Mary. He spoke to Paul. He spoke to Peter. Flip through the pages of church history, and you find men and women who have trained the inner ear to hear the voice of God and have ordered their lives around what they have heard.

> Flip through the pages of church history, and you find men and women who have trained the inner ear to hear the voice of God.

Even Jesus centered his ministry around hearing the voice of God. "The Son can do nothing by himself," he said. "He can only do what he sees his Father doing. . . . For the Father loves the Son and shows him all he does" (John 5:19–20).

He will show us, too—if we learn to listen.

∽

Word and power churches teach their people to listen to the talking God. They impart a ravenous hunger for the Scriptures where the living Word intrudes prophetically into the details of our lives. And they stir up an eagerness for the prophetic gifts, which strengthen, encourage, and comfort.

Study Questions

1. Having no time for "theological banter" in seminary also meant, in retrospect, no time for reflection. What has been your experience with spiritual reflection? How has this book helped you to address issues that have puzzled you?

2. "When you pare away the externals that distract us, charismatics and evangelicals are basically saying the same thing about how God speaks." Do you agree or disagree with this statement? What are the implications of this?

3. Is it difficult for you to accept the "genius of the AND" when it comes to your understanding of how God speaks today?

4. Discuss the four steps toward becoming a healthy church. How balanced is your church in each of these areas? What are some specific ways you can encourage growth in those areas of imbalance?

CHAPTER EIGHT

NOT ALL SPEAK IN TONGUES, DO THEY?

I knew that Janey prayed with a prayer language, and I asked her to relate how she received it.

"My daughter was very, very sick, and I was not handling it well. One night I drove up and down Cherokee Boulevard until I finally found myself parked by the water. I wished I could have driven into it. I was at a real point of despair. God really rescued me there. . . . It was as if he came into my car, came into the deepest part of me, and I began to pray." God gave Janey a phrase that night in a language not her own. Over the coming months, she prayed the phrase in her times with the Lord.

Several years passed. Janey became friends with a young woman emerging from satanic ritual abuse. Hours of counseling and prayer seemed to have little impact on her friend's damaged soul. Then, one Saturday morning in the fall of 1995, Janey and several others gathered to begin what became a marathon counseling session with her friend. The morning quietly slipped away, and two o'clock found a frustrated ministry team and a worn-out young woman sprawled across Janey's living room amidst half-eaten sandwiches, cold cups of coffee, dog-eared Neal Anderson books, and several Bibles. Janey went to her bedroom for a break.

"I began to really seek God, to really seek the power of prayer. My prayers felt so powerless! I wasn't really seeking a prayer language, just more of him." Janey lay on her bed, weary from the battle that was still raging downstairs. And then it happened.

"I put a Twila Paris tape on and was trying to clear my head. Then I heard a phrase—different from the one I learned at the river—in an inaudible voice. I listened and then began to pray the phrase back to God. I knew then I was praying in tongues."

Janey prayed that phrase for several years. It sounded like Hebrew to her, but she couldn't translate it. During the fall of 1997 she attended a conference on prayer in Charlotte, North Carolina, with several friends who had been drawn together by a shared passion for the nation of Vietnam. The conference concluded with a powerful moment of repentance and reconciliation. The speaker, who had been teaching on the topic of identificational repentance in the Old Testament, asked for one man from Vietnam to come to the platform to stand for the nation of Vietnam. A former GI who had served in Vietnam then joined them on the platform. The GI asked the Vietnamese brother to forgive him. The Vietnamese man did, and a tremendous release of emotion swept through the crowd.

Janey sensed God telling her that now was the time when she was going to learn what her phrase means. She went to the worship leader and said, "I believe God has given me a phrase in Hebrew to pray, but I'm not sure what it means. Can you interpret it for me?"

"No," he said. "But I know someone who can."

The worship leader introduced Janey to Dr. Gary S. Greig, who was then associate professor of Hebrew and Old Testament at Regent University in Virginia and who is currently professor of biblical languages and Old Testament with the Wagner Leadership Institute in Colorado Springs. Dr. Greig has a Ph.D. in Near Eastern Languages from the University of Chicago and "just happened" to be standing by the platform where the Vietnamese and American brother had just stood on behalf of their nations. Janey wrote out the phrase. Dr. Greig looked at it carefully and then translated it. "It means in Hebrew, 'A man for the nations.'"

"That's what just happened," Janey replied. "Those two men represented their nations in repentance."

"You're right," Dr. Greig answered.

"I felt so loved by God at that point. All I could do was praise him for everything he is," Janey told me later.

God used that moment to refine Janey's calling to pray for Vietnam. A year later, she joined a prayer team and spent two weeks praying throughout Vietnam. Today she provides vital prayer support for Fellowship's Vietnamese church-planting team. And yes, her prayer language, which is no longer just one phrase, is a significant part of her ministry tool kit.

Most who know Janey would know little, if anything, about this part of her life. "I hold it closely," she says. "It's a very intimate, personal gift." For Janey, spiritual language is a gift that helps her experience Christ's love for her and her love for him. "It's part of the marriage between the bride and the Bridegroom. We share this prayer together. I find myself opening up more and more to him."

What Do We Do with Janey's Story?

Stories like Janey's are charged with spiritual power. They demand a response, but too often, it's the wrong one. One type of wrong response runs something like this: "See! Spiritual language is the key to intimacy with Christ and the release of spiritual power. Everyone must have this spiritual gift."

For many years, this has been the position of the Pentecostal and charismatic churches. Their own encounter with the gift of tongues has been so significant in their spiritual journey that they naturally want everyone to enjoy what they have enjoyed. They have seen that the coming of the Spirit can be witnessed in the book of Acts by speaking in tongues, and they have viewed these descriptions as normative—what every believer should experience.

This stance is softening, however. Today many charismatics believe that the gift of spiritual language is not the only evidence of the Spirit-filled life; they acknowledge that many in the body of Christ enjoy deep intimacy with Christ and a dynamic prayer life without it. Jack Hayford, pastor of the Church on the Way in Van Nuys, California, took a brave and kind step in his landmark book, *The Beauty of Spiritual Language,* when he wrote, "There are too many people I know who are living power-filled lives under the touch of the gifts of the Holy Spirit, though never having spoken with tongues."[1] Hayford, a Pentecostal, believes tongues are "a provision for all believers—for prayer and praise."[2] But in allowing the possibility for a believer to not have this gift and still live an empowered life, he has built a bridge of grace between the two traditions that many will walk over.

The Bible clearly teaches that not everyone will speak in tongues. Paul ends 1 Corinthians 12 by asking a series of rhetorical questions:

"Do all work miracles? . . . Do all speak in tongues? Do all interpret?" (v. 29–30). The answer he clearly expects is no.

Church history supports this as well. I have ransacked the historical accounts for evidence of speaking in tongues—what the scholars call *glossalalia*. You can find some evidence of the charismatic gifts, including spiritual languages, scattered across the centuries—but not much. For some reason, God did not choose to give the gift of spiritual language to large numbers of his people until the beginning of the twentieth century. Different people have different theories about why this is so. But it is important to point out that many of the church's greatest saints over the past two millennia never spoke in tongues. Does anybody really want to say that Martin Luther, John Calvin, Charles Spurgeon, D. L. Moody, or Amy Carmichael were not empowered by the Holy Spirit because they never spoke in tongues? I doubt it.

> You can find some evidence of the charismatic gifts, including spiritual languages, scattered across the centuries — but not much.

My own pastoral experience supports this thought as well. Some of the godliest people in our church have a spiritual language, but some of them do not. Some of my elders pray in a spiritual language, and some of them do not. Some of my staff pray in a spiritual language, yet some of them do not. We have learned to love one another and allow God to give us whatever gifts he wants.

The other type of wrong response takes the knife and cuts the other way: "I have never had that kind of experience, and I don't think anybody else should either." The evangelical resistance to spiritual language is softening, however. As early as 1973, an editorial in the evangelical magazine *Eternity* observed, "More and more evangelical scholars today feel that the traditional, supposed biblical arguments for cessation of the gifts after completion of the New Testament cannot be sustained by the Holy Scripture. . . . The new stress is on the church as the body of Christ with its various members endowed by the Spirit with different gifts. . . . and who would rule out tongues as one of these gifts? Certainly Paul didn't."[3] It has been a long time since I met an evangelical leader younger than I who believes that God would never give this gift today.

One afternoon in my office I pointed some verses out to a dear friend and faithful leader who was convinced that spiritual language is wrong: "I would like every one of you to speak in tongues" (1 Cor. 14:5), and, "I speak in tongues more than all of you" (v. 18).

"But tongues are selfish!" he said, trying to keep the edge off his words.

"Where do you see that?" I replied, trying to keep the edge off my words.

"Right here. Verse 4! 'He who speaks in a tongue edifies himself.' Tongues is selfish."

We didn't go much further that day. Later I went back and considered his concern. Is it really selfish to edify yourself? The word *edify* means to build up. I want to build others up. But I have to build myself up to be strong enough to minister to others. I do use my spiritual gifts to edify myself. I use my teaching gift to mine truths from the Word to edify myself. I use my discernment gift to search my own soul for sin. Scripture even *commands* us to build ourselves up. Jude tells us, "Dear friends, build yourselves up in your most holy faith" (Jude 20).

I came to the conclusion that most scholars have come to—that Paul is not condemning tongues in 1 Corinthians 14 but teaching us how to use the gift in a loving way.

Whether we like it or not, Paul is forcing us to live in tension. He speaks warmly about the gift of spiritual language and then says everyone doesn't receive this gift. We don't like ambiguity and paradox in our theology, so we form entire movements around half-truths. It's easier that way. It's also wrong. Today 540 million people claim to be either Pentecostal or charismatic Christians. Does anybody really want to argue that the tremendous explosion of the power church in the late twentieth century is not of God? Some 1.5 billion Christians are considered evangelical. Does anybody really want to say that none of them are experiencing the Spirit-filled life because they haven't spoken in tongues?

> We don't like ambiguity and paradox in our theology, so we form entire movements around half-truths. It's easier that way. It's also wrong.

D. Martyn Lloyd-Jones honors the tension in the biblical teaching about gifts like spiritual language when he writes, "We must not say 'only' for New Testament times nor must we say 'always.' The answer is, 'as he wills,' as the Spirit wills. . . . the gifts of the Spirit are to be left in the hands of the Holy Spirit himself."[4]

WHAT IS SPIRITUAL LANGUAGE?

Spiritual language is the best contemporary term used to describe what most translations call "the gift of tongues." Paul wrote as a pastor, not a linguist, so we do not find an analysis of spiritual language in his letters. But we are treated to some hints: Spiritual language is like the language of angels, it is prayer to God, and it can bring words from God to us. Spiritual language is a language of prayer and praise.

The Greek word for *tongue* is *glossa*. It can mean the tongue in your mouth, or it can mean language. Our grandparents used to speak of a foreign language as a foreign *tongue,* but that use has passed away. Today we study foreign languages in college, not foreign tongues.

Language is the currency of relationship. I spent a day recently in the stacks of Hodges Library at the University of Tennessee in search of a good definition of language. Five hours later, in exasperation, I called a friend who is a speech therapist working with children. She gave me a book much more on my level called *The New Language of Toys.* Big print. Lots of pictures. I knew I was getting close. "Language is the way we explain our feelings," the book explains. "How could we express our deepest emotions without language? Fear, happiness, and sadness are all communicated using language. All through life people use language in forming relationships, expressing love, and sharing thoughts and feelings."[5]

I surveyed a number of people in my congregation to find out why they prayed in a prayer language and what benefit it gave them. Some described the emotional benefit. Others spoke of the intimacy they experienced with Christ. Still others said it drew them into the Word. Their responses fit surprisingly easily within the definition in *The New Language of Toys.*

Spiritual language is a way of expressing feelings and emotions, a way of connecting with happiness, fear, and sadness. Spiritual language helps us as God's children to nurture our relationship with Jesus, express our love to him, and share thoughts and feelings that are hard to express.

Language is made up of words. When two people exchange words, what happens—to use the words of Eugene Peterson—is that "revelation takes place and relationship becomes intimate."[6]

Walter Ong, who has spent an academic lifetime pondering the essence of words, says a word is "the call of one interior . . . to another interior."[7] In other words, a word is an expression of a deep part of me that connects with a deep part of you. Words are sacred, intimate things.

When we begin to reflect more deeply on what language really is—the intimate communion of my heart with your heart, laced with mystery, impossible to define, leading into intimacy and under-standing and oneness—it is easier to see spiritual language for what it is: a gift of spiritual words that links my heart to God's heart, my passion to his passion. These are words from lover to beloved, from the "deep interior" of my con-sciousness into the deep interior of his.

> It is easier to see spiritual language for what it is: a gift of spiritual words that links my heart to God's heart, my passion to his passion.

Jesus tells us that his kingdom is not of this world. The Sermon on the Mount paints in stark colors the contrast be-tween his value system and the value system of the world. We follow a new king who is building a new kingdom. Should it surprise us that this kingdom also has a new language?

The strange thing is that some citizens of this kingdom are given this new language and some are not. Why?

It has something to do with love.

THE GREATEST OF THESE IS LOVE

Some time ago, a concerned member of a vibrant, dynamic young church wrote the founding pastor a letter. The letter went something like this:

> Dear pastor,
> I have a question about spiritual language. How impor-tant is it to my spiritual life? Some seem to think it is the key to a satisfying spiritual life. I'm not so sure. At any rate, there is some tension in our church family right now about this gift. Some of us seem to emphasize it too much. Others want to forbid it altogether because it causes so much trouble. What should we do?

The letter I just paraphrased for you was written nearly two thou-sand years ago by some members of the church of Corinth to the apos-tle Paul, who had planted the church several years earlier. Today the letter is known as "the lost letter" because we don't have a copy of it. Paul wrote his first letter to the Corinthians in response to this lost letter. The Corinthians were about to experience the first charismatic-evangelical church split. Paul wisely shepherded them through the storm, and he did so by reframing the question. They wanted to know about tongues. He wanted to talk to them about love.

Here is the heart of Paul's teaching:

> If I speak in the tongues of men and of angels, but have not love, I am only a resounding gong or a clanging cymbal. . . .
> Love is patient, love is kind. It does not envy, it does not boast, it is not proud. It is not rude, it is not self-seeking, it is not easily angered, it keeps no record of wrongs. Love does not delight in evil but rejoices with the truth. It always protects, always trusts, always hopes, always perseveres. (1 Cor. 13:1, 4–7)

Paul's eulogy to love has been the sermon text at thousands of Christian weddings, but he was not talking specifically about marriage. His eloquent words have been cross-stitched, done in needlepoint, embossed, and displayed on everything from birthday cards to calendars. Yet we have forgotten why he wrote the words in the first place—to teach people who speak in tongues and people who don't speak in tongues how to get along.

Paul's point is simple: It is more important that I love you than that I speak in tongues.

God created the body of Christ with great diversity (Paul's message in 1 Corinthians 12). We are like a body, each of us being a different body part and all interdependent. We need each other. But getting along as a body is no easy task, requiring large dosages of supernatural love (Paul's message in 1 Corinthians 13). Love means we learn to limit our freedoms and use our gifts in ways that build up, instead of tear down, our brothers and sisters in the body (Paul's message in 1 Corinthians 14).

> God delights in diversity. Humans tend to find it a problem.

God delights in diversity. Humans tend to find it a problem. So instead of following the law of love, we tear the body apart. All the eyes can meet in one church. All the ears can meet in another. We find those who are just like us so we don't have to do the hard work of love.

That's what has happened among charismatics and evangelicals in the twentieth century. We haven't wanted to learn to love each other, so we have gone our separate ways, building our separate kingdoms and each of us missing the whole point of 1 Corinthians 12–14: *love*. Jack Deere assesses the damage:

> Somewhere along the way . . . the church has encouraged a silent divorce between the Word and the Spirit. Divorces are painful, both for the children and the parents. One parent usually gets custody of the children, and the other gets to visit occasionally. It breaks the hearts of the parents, and the children are usually worse off because of the arrangement. Many in the church today are content to live with only one parent. They live with the Word, and the Spirit has only limited visiting rights. He just gets to see and touch the kids once in a while. Some of his kids don't even recognize him anymore. Some have become afraid of him. Others in the church live with the Spirit and only allow the Word sporadic visits. The Spirit doesn't want to raise the kids without the Word. He can see how unruly they're becoming, but he won't force them to do what they must choose in their hearts.
>
> So the church has become a divided family growing up with separate parents. One set of kids is proud of their education, and the other set of kids is proud of their freedom. Both think they're better than the other.
>
> The parents are brokenhearted. Because unlike most divorces, they didn't choose this divorce. Their kids did. And the Word and the Spirit have had to honor and endure that choice.[8]

God's heart must be breaking, because his message is one of reconciliation, of bringing together that which sin has torn apart. "All this is from God, who reconciled us to himself through Christ and gave us the ministry of reconciliation" (2 Cor. 5:18). "For he himself is our peace, who has made the two one and has destroyed the barrier" (Eph. 2:14). "You are all sons of God through faith in Christ Jesus. . . . There is neither Jew nor Greek, slave nor free, male nor female, for you are all one in Christ Jesus" (Gal. 3:26–28).

What message do we have for a world splitting in two if we ourselves are not one? How can we preach a gospel of reconciliation when we ourselves are not reconciled? What shall I say to an anguished young couple, teetering on the abyss of divorce, after adultery is confessed? How can I tell them to forgive, press on, reconcile in a broken marriage if I cannot even convince believers who have different prayer styles to stay together?

> God is calling us beyond tolerance, beyond even acceptance, into total reconciliation and oneness.

Here is the good news: The civil spiritual wars of a generation ago now seem to have died down. Evangelicals, watching the explosion of the charismatic movement around the world, are taking seriously a movement that is leading fifty-four thousand people a day to Christ.[9]

Charismatics, finding themselves invited back to the family table, are accepting the invitation. The first stage in the "peace talks" between the two camps took place in the seventies and eighties. God raised up the Vineyard movement, which blends evangelical and charismatic teaching, and the "Third Wave" movement, which consists of evangelical believers who want to walk in all the gifts but remain in their evangelical denominations. A spirit of tolerance began to set in.

Now, at the dawn of a new millennium, God is calling us beyond tolerance, beyond even acceptance, into total reconciliation and oneness. He is calling the two halves of the churches back together again, not just to endure one another, but to delight in one another's uniqueness and profit from it.

God is calling us to a higher level of unity than ever before. He is asking us to embrace the full diversity of the body of Christ. And God's people are responding.

SIGNS FROM SAIGON

On our final night in Saigon, a special visitor appeared at our dinner table whom we will call Mr. Li. He was a leader in the underground Vietnamese house church movement and wanted to share his story with us. Mr. Li had been actively involved with the evangelical movement that the communists had consolidated into one state church after Saigon fell in 1975. During the early eighties, many Vietnamese believers began praying fervently for revival. God soon answered their prayers, but not exactly the way they thought he would. Some churches experiencing a fresh touch of God's power during the revival also began to experience some of the so-called charismatic gifts we considered in chapter 7. Turmoil erupted in the churches. Eventually the charismatics felt they had to leave the evangelical church. There was nowhere else for them to go legally, so they went underground, birthing a house-church movement that is now ninety thousand churches strong.

Mr. Li's story doesn't end there. We stole away into a nearby hotel room to talk more frankly about what God was doing in Mr. Li's country and to pray. "We need each other," our new friend whispered softly. "God is at work in both groups. It is time to work together."

IT IS TIME TO WORK TOGETHER

It *is* time to work together, and many churches are doing so. Fellowship Church is one of them.

I have thought often about the quote from F. Scott Fitzgerald that Professor Collins uses in *Built to Last*: "The test of a first-rate intelligence is the ability to hold two opposed ideas in the mind at the same time, and still retain the ability to function." There have been times on our journey into a word and power church when retaining the ability to function has been quite difficult. But we are learning—and growing. I want to end this chapter by sharing with you some of the lessons learned along the way.

IT'S ALL ABOUT LOVE

The bottom line is love. Our rule of thumb has been, "When in doubt, love." Paul fleshes out the principle this way: "Let us therefore make every effort to do what leads to peace and to mutual edification. . . . Each of us should please his neighbor for his good, to build him up" (Rom. 14:19; 15:2). This is the only law that is needed. It covers every possible circumstance. I simply ask the question: "Will this build up my brother or sister?" If the answer is no, then I limit my liberty for the sake of my brother or sister.

Different churches will apply the law of love differently. Fellowship Church draws many people from conservative evangelical backgrounds, many from mainline churches, and some who have not been in church for many years. We want our Sunday celebration service to be a safe place where they can be led "beyond religion into relationship with Jesus." Our elders have concluded, after much prayer, study, and fasting, that allowing public praying in spiritual language in the worship service might in many cases not be loving toward our guests. We ask those who have this gifting to limit their liberty to use this gift in the celebration service.

We have chosen, given our mission, to focus our time on worship, the preaching of the Word, and post-service prayer ministry. (We currently have four services each Sunday, with seventy-five minutes per service.) We chose to limit our liberty to pray in spiritual language publicly for another reason. Nearly three thousand people attend our services each Sunday; the elders do not know all of them. Scripture challenges elders to guard the flock. We are concerned that if we let anyone pray in a spiritual language and if we let anyone interpret, we might be exposing our flock to influence from people whose character is not known to us.

Are we quenching the Spirit by limiting people's liberty this way? We don't think so. Remember, the goal is love, not the freedom to use our gifts. We are more concerned to love the people than to make sure someone with a prayer language can use his or her gift. Actually, we ask many other people also to limit the use of their gifts during the celebration services—we ask many encouragers not to encourage, many administrators not to administrate, and many teachers not to teach—but then provide other ways for them to use their gifts.

You will need to determine what most builds up your congregation. Remember, the purpose of every spiritual gift is the edification of the body. If a gift doesn't edify, God isn't in it.

> The purpose of every spiritual gift is the edification of the body. If a gift doesn't edify, God isn't in it.

Every Christian needs a place to grow in his or her spiritual gifts. I have spent years in schools and in my study refining my teaching gift. The same is true with the gifts mentioned in 1 Corinthians 12: We need a place to practice them. The small group is a safe place to practice spiritual gifts. Mistakes will be made, but any damage is easier to control in a small group. It is easier to recover and grow and receive correction in an environment where you know you are loved and accepted.

We don't emphasize any particular gift in our small-group training. We don't forbid any gift, either. Again, the guiding rule is love. We train the group leaders to train their people to use their gifts in a way that builds everyone else up. We ask those who have a prayer language and are led to pray aloud in their small group to ask themselves, "Will this build up my brothers and sisters, or will it hurt them?" Typically, a person who is led to pray in a prayer language will ask permission from the group if this is a new experience for the group. The person might say, "God has given me a prayer language, and I feel led to pray now and ask God for interpretation from the group. Would that offend anyone in any way?"

Spiritual language plays a significant role in some of Fellowship's small groups, especially the ones that focus on prayer. Generally, someone prays in his or her language and another interprets. The interpretations are never introduced with the words "Thus says the Lord," for the reasons we examined in chapter 7. They are normally gentle, shepherding words encouraging specific needs occurring in the group that night.

The word *interpret* (NRSV) means *to explain* (NIV). It doesn't necessarily mean *to translate*. Luke uses the word *interpret* in describing how Jesus taught the Old Testament to the disciples on the road to Emmaus (Luke 24). Jesus didn't translate the entire Old Testament for them, but he gave them the sense of its meaning. Spiritual language with interpretation is a type of prophetic ministry. God speaks through the tongue and interpretation. Of course, this message is not seen as divinely authoritative and needs to be weighed against Scripture and wise counsel.

Recently it became clear to me that a close friend was being called to the mission field. I want more than anything for Fellowship to be a sending church, but it hurts when people go! I was surprised at how deeply hurt I felt at the potential letting go of my friend. During a small-group meeting where we were praying for my friend, someone also prayed in a spiritual language for me. Another interpreted. I wrote the interpretation down in my journal:

> Doug, your grief is real. You must give him up to me. Release him to the calling I have for him. Many will try to hold him back. Many will try to keep him. Don't be one. Don't be grieved. Mine is the better way.

God comforted me that night through this gift.

Most of our small groups do not regularly practice the gift of spiritual language, yet their members experience great comfort, intimate prayer, and encouragement from the Word.

We stress to the small-group leaders the Spirit's sovereignty in distributing his gifts. No group is more spiritual than any other because of the gifts it does or does not practice.

At Fellowship Church, the gift of spiritual language is most commonly practiced in private as a means of personal prayer and praise. It is not really a topic of discussion, and we don't have a lot of people praying for one another to receive this gift. The Spirit in his sovereignty seems to grace certain of his people with this gift in their private times with him—as he did with Janey, and as he did with me. Those who receive the gift tend to keep it a private matter between themselves and God.

Your church will need to decide what is the most loving way to embrace those who pray in a spiritual language and to honor those who do not. The way we are doing it is not necessarily the way you should do it. Just remember this:

The Spirit is sovereign.

And the greatest priority is love.

Study Questions

1. What was your initial response to Janey's story? After reflection, how do you respond to it?

2. If the doctrine of cessation is an issue for you, spend some time discussing appendix 1.

3. Have you ever been given the gift of tongues? If not, do you desire that gift? Why or why not?

4. If members of your church were given a spiritual language, how would your church respond? If members of your church were not given a spiritual language, how would your church respond? How can you promote acceptance of both?

5. "When in doubt, love." Does this rule characterize your church?

CHAPTER NINE

WE NEED THE CABOOSE

I love *The Four Spiritual Laws*—that wonderfully simple explanation of the gospel, developed by Campus Crusade's Bill Bright
in the sixties to make it easy for folks like me to share their faith.
I have given away hundreds of copies of *The Four Spiritual Laws*
and keep one copy in my wallet and several in my briefcase.

Law 1: God loves you and has a wonderful plan for your life.

Law 2: Man is sinful and separated from God. Therefore, he
cannot know and experience God's love and plan for his life.

Law 3: Jesus Christ is God's only provision for man's sin.
Through Him you can know and experience God's love and
plan for your life.

Law 4: We must individually receive Jesus Christ as Savior
and Lord; then we can know and experience God's love and
plan for our lives.

Tucked away in the back of the tract is a one-page discussion on
the role of feelings in the spiritual life. It begins like this: "An important reminder ... **Do Not Depend on Feelings.** The promise of
God's Word, the Bible—not our feelings—is our authority." Then
below is the famous train diagram. The engine is called the fact car.
The car behind the engine is the faith car. And the caboose is the
feelings car. "The train will run with or without the caboose. However, it will be useless to attempt to pull the train by the caboose. In

the same way, as Christians we do not depend on feelings or emotions, but we place our faith [trust] in the trustworthiness of God and the promises of His Word."

I know what Dr. Bright is saying: Feelings are optional in the Christian life. Actually, they are kind of scary and may get you into trouble—so don't depend on them.

Contemplating on this after reading it for the first time, my mind wandered to Jesus' command to "love the Lord your God with all your heart and . . . with all your mind" (Mark 12:30). Could this primarily be a command to *obey* Jesus? After all, Jesus did say, "If you love me, you will obey what I command" (John 14:15). Loving Jesus, I concluded, is obeying Jesus. And as for feelings? Well, the train doesn't need the caboose.

My understanding of loving Jesus as obeying Jesus was reinforced in seminary. My seminary professors had a deep reverence for the holy Scriptures and imparted a sacred fear of "wrongly dividing them" (as the King James Version puts it in 2 Timothy 2:15). (I suppose that's why I find myself up late so many Saturday nights finishing a sermon or even writing a new one—because I am terrified of wrongly dividing the Word.) One of the implicit lessons I learned in seminary was "don't drag your own issues into the Word. Let the Word speak to you." We were trained to keep our own biases, thoughts, and feelings distant from a careful study of the text. Once the text's meaning was made plain, then we could apply it to our lives. My goal became learning how to unearth principles from God's Word and present them in such a way that people could obey them.

I took this conviction with me into the church we planted. I believed my primary task as the shepherd of the flock was to help people learn biblical principles and then to call them to obey.

The seminars I went to in those days illustrate this approach to loving God. The notebooks I brought home from the seminars are filled with principles, most of which are wonderfully alliterated, that we were to obey. A great seminar boiled down the mysteries of life to five key points, six central lessons, or four crucial truths. Religious feelings didn't play a part in these conferences.

Looking back on it, I perceive another reason why I didn't trust the "feelings" caboose. I am not a very feeling-oriented person, nor were most of my friends. The only feelings I was intimately acquainted with were sexual ones. If I felt anything deeply, it was the tug of lust. During my seminary days, several prominent Christian leaders committed adultery and lost their ministries. Three of them had spoken on our campus at one time or another. So when they fell, I was devastated.

Bill Bright was right, I concluded. Don't trust the caboose. We can't run our life by feelings; we have to base our life on the facts of God's Word even when our feelings say otherwise.

My cabooseless spirituality worked for a while—until the engine started to run out of fuel. As I related in an earlier chapter, I soon found that there is more to loving God than obeying him. (Not less, but more.) For the first time in my life I began to yearn for spiritual emotion. I began to wonder if there was more to loving than obeying.

My foray into the charismatic world was driven, in part, by a quest for spiritual feelings. My encounter in the cabin when I received the new spiritual language from God was the first time ever I had felt *anything* in my spiritual life. And I liked it.

> For the first time in my life I began to yearn for spiritual emotion. I began to wonder if there was more to loving than obeying.

The charismatic world I intersected was anything but afraid of the feeling caboose. In fact, in some cases, the feeling caboose drove the train. Whatever else I might say about my charismatic friends, they did *feel* something for Jesus that I did not. This was a world where emotions were not the enemy of faith but the source of it. People laughed. People cried. People shook. People were slain in the Spirit. People danced. People lay on the floor praying.

Much of what I saw seemed sincere—a genuine interaction with a living God. Over the years I have become good friends with several charismatic and Pentecostal pastors. I know their hearts. They are not faking things, nor do they permit their people to. I have visited with Pentecostal theologians, traveled to revival services, and chatted with graduate students training to serve in charismatic churches. In nearly every case I have come away sensing that the Spirit of God was truly involved in who they were and what they were doing.

I also found, though, that a caboose-driven faith has some drawbacks. Sometimes emotions seemed to be worked up rather than genuine. I would meet people who had emotional encounters week after week, but never really seemed to change. Some of these people seemed addicted to the *experience* of a spiritual encounter. In some cases, I found a near disdain for careful study of the Word. Solid preaching and hard doctrinal digging were synonyms for dry, lifeless orthodoxy.

Once again I was thrust into paradox, compelled to search for the genius of the AND. Was there no way to have a principled, obedient faith *and* a deeply emotional spirituality? Is there a way to love God with all your heart *and* all your mind?

God sent a messenger to teach me how to bring the two worlds together. His name is Jonathan Edwards.

NOTHING NEW UNDER THE SUN

Revival swept the American colonies in the 1730s, and with it came painful controversy. Sometimes the revival meetings were marked with strange emotional phenomena the colonists had never seen before. As we noted earlier, Edwards was so cautious about falsely stirring emotion that he read his sermons in a monotone behind thick glasses. Yet his famous sermon *Sinners in the Hands of an Angry God,* for example, was received with wailing, tears, and abject terror.

George Whitefield, a contemporary of Edwards, was not so careful. Drawing on his training as an actor, he stirred crowds into a frenzy with his dramatic oratory. Some Christians delighted in the revival and welcomed the emotionalism with great fervor. People traveled long distances to the revival meetings, hoping for a touch from God.

Other Christians felt the whole movement was of the devil. They called for a return to the quieter, more intellectual faith New England had been known for. Great controversy broke out among the leading pastors and theologians of the day.

Edwards rose up amid the controversy with a book, *Religious Affections,* that today, 250 years after it came from the theologian's quill pen, towers over everything else written on the subject. It is a brilliant example of embracing the genius of the AND.

Edwards refused to take sides. He refused to condemn either emotionalism or doctrine-based preaching. With great wisdom he reframed the question around the matter of affections for Jesus. (We would use the word *passion* for his word *affection.*) Edwards argued that true spirituality is a passionate spirituality marked by obedient living. Loving God, Edwards declared, involves both emotion and obedience.

I first read *Religious Affections* six years ago. The first chapter changed my life forever. I want to dust off this classic and share with you some highlights from Edwards's study. His time-honored principles serve as a blueprint for the word and power church as we try to wed emotion and obedience into one holy passion for Jesus. I will modernize some of the words to make his work easier to understand. You owe it to yourself to read the original sometime.

WHY TRUE SPIRITUALITY IS PASSIONATE SPIRITUALITY

The Bible commands passion. "God," says Edwards, "in His word, greatly insists that we be in good earnest, 'fervent in spirit,' and our hearts vigorously engaged in religion." In the same way, Paul demands, "Never be lacking in zeal, but keep your spiritual fervor" (Rom. 12:11). God pleads through Moses, "Love the LORD your God with all your heart and with all your soul and with all your strength" (Deut. 6:5). Our hearts should "burn within us" when we walk with Christ, just as the disciples' hearts were set ablaze when they walked with him on the road to Emmaus (Luke 24:32).

Passions are the power of life. Our passions motivate us. Edwards writes, "Take away all love and hatred, all hope and fear, all anger, zeal and affectionate desire, and the world would be . . . motionless and dead." The same is true in the spiritual life. We will not be led to do great works for God if we are not passionately in love with God. Merely knowing facts about God won't do it. "He that has doctrinal knowledge and speculation only, without affection, never is engaged in the business of religion."

> Edwards's time-honored principles serve as a blueprint . . . as we try to wed emotion and obedience into one holy passion for Jesus.

Passion provokes life change. People don't leave their sin and move toward God without their hearts first being touched and melted by God's love. This holds true for sinners: "Nor was ever one induced to fly for refuge unto Christ, while his heart remained unaffected." It is also true for saints: "Nor was there ever a saint awakened out of a cold, lifeless frame, or recovered from a declining state in religion, and brought back from a lamentable departure from God, without having his heart affected." We must stir passion in people if people are to change.

Scripture describes true spirituality as passionate spirituality. Consider the terms the Bible uses when it talks about the kinds of passions that ought naturally to stir in every believer's heart. We are to *fear* God. We are to have great *hope* in the Lord. We are to *hate* sin. We are to *thirst* after God's presence, as a deer pants after water. We are to taste holy *joy*. We are to know *sorrow, mourning, and brokenness* of heart. We should experience deep *gratitude* and overwhelming *compassion*. Our lives should be marked by burning *zeal*. "They who would deny that much of true religion lies in the affections . . . must throw away . . . our Bible."

Scripture teaches that love, which is the greatest passion, is the essence of our faith. We are to love God with everything we have and love our neighbor as ourselves. Love is the heart of all passions. Love gives birth to all the other passions. We hate sin because we love God. We delight in righteousness because we love God. We grieve over our sin because we love God. We have compassion toward our brother and sister because we love the God who made them.

Our Bible heroes model a passionate spirituality. David, who was "a man after God's own heart," displays a passionate heart for God in the Psalms. "Those holy songs of his . . . are nothing else but the expressions and breathings of devout and holy affections." This should tell us something about how God longs for passionate followers, because the Psalms were intended to guide God's people in worship and praise.

Paul offers another good example. Edwards writes, "It appears by all [Paul's] expressions of himself, that he was, in the course of his life, inflamed and entirely swallowed up by a most ardent love to his glorious Lord, esteeming all things as loss, for the excellency of knowing Him." Paul was overpowered by holy passion, and it compelled him to press on in ministry amid great suffering. His letters are scattered with expressions of tender love for his people. His heart ached when he thought of how his own people, the Jews, resisted the gospel.

We must not overlook John. His writings "breathe nothing but the most fervent love, as though he were all made up of sweet and holy affection." To provide all the evidence supporting Edwards's statement would mean copying all of his writings into this book!

**Jesus himself is the perfect example of a deeply passion-
ate spirituality.** "The Lord Jesus Christ was a Person who was
remarkably of a tender and affectionate heart; and His virtue was
expressed very much in the exercise of holy affections. He was the
greatest instance of ardency, vigor, and strength of love to both God
and man, that ever was." Jesus prayed with tears and wrestling and
blood. He was sorrowful even to the point of death. His zeal for his
Father's house consumed him. His anger for the hard-hearted religious professionals boiled. His compassion for his cherished
Jerusalem seeped out of him in weeping.

The religion of heaven is very passionate. "According to the
scriptural representation of the heavenly state, the religion of heaven
consists chiefly in holy and mighty love and joy, and the expression
of these in most fervent and exalted praises."

God gives his church practices that stir passion. God tells
us to sing praises to him for no other reason than "to excite and
express religious affections." The same is true with communion. God
knew that we needed more than just to hear about the redemption
of Christ. We needed to see something, to touch something, if our
passions were to remain stirred. Let's not forget the preaching of the
Word. Why preach the Word? One great reason is because the Word,
when preached with power, stirs passion for God.

**The Scriptures declare that the great sin is a hard and pas-
sionless heart.** Jesus grieved over the hard hearts of the Jews. Paul
told the Romans that the wrath of God would come upon the hardened of heart. The prophets cried out against the danger of a hard
heart. "Now by a hard heart is plainly meant an unaffected heart, or
a heart not easy to be moved by virtuous affections, like a stone,
insensible, stupid, unmoved, and hard to be impressed."

✍

Edwards ends his chapter by drawing three conclusions as to the
implications of passionate spirituality:

**1. If true spirituality is passionate spirituality, we shouldn't
condemn fervent spiritual passion just because some have
abused it.** True, there were abuses in the great revival, some three
or four years before Edwards wrote these words. "We easily run from
one extreme to another." At that time people thought that all passion
was good passion. Now they are saying that any display of spiritual

passion is a bad thing. The truth is somewhere in the middle. "As there is no true religion where there is nothing else but affection, so there is not true religion where there is no religious affection."

2. If true spirituality is a passionate spirituality, we should "infer that such means are to be desired as have much of a tendency to move the affections." Edwards continues, "Such books, and such a way as preaching the Word, and administering ordinances, and such a way of worshipping God in prayer, and singing praises, is much to be desired, as have a tendency deeply to affect the heart."

3. If true spirituality is fervent spirituality, we should be ashamed by how passionless we are. People are passionate about many things—their honor, their reputation, their businesses, their friendships. This should embarrass us when we consider how little passion we have for the great things of God. Is there anyone more worthy of passionate pursuit than Jesus?

↳⊃

How do we know if someone's passion is truly of the Spirit and not merely contrived emotionalism? By watching that person's life. Genuine passion always results in an obedient life. An obedient, holy life is, as Edwards says, "the chief sign of grace." Jesus said, "By their fruit you will recognize them" (Matt. 7:16).

> Genuine passion always results in an obedient life.

Many people talk about their religion. But "words are cheap; and godliness is more easily feigned in words than in actions. Christian practice is a costly, laborious thing." Genuine spiritual passion leads to genuine Christian living.

THE LIBRARY

God led me to Jonathan Edwards just when I needed him most. The object of Edwards's brilliant biblical portrayal—that normal spirituality is intensely passionate spirituality—became my goal.

During the year I spent in counseling, my counselor and I probed some of the causes of my burnout. A metaphor emerged that helped me understand my inner world and my lack of passion. My inner world is like a library. It is a quiet, comfortable place with hundreds of well-loved books lining oak shelves. A plushy couch, several reading chairs, and a table covered with magazines and newspapers completes the picture. I like this library. It's a safe place—well-ordered, comfortable, and impeccably orthodox.

My counselor and I prayed about this image and gradually realized that it was a perfect description of my faith. My faith was centered in knowledge—orthodox knowledge. My faith was well-ordered and reasonable. It was comfortable. And it worked. Or at least it did until the spring of 1997.

We prayed some more. Another metaphor came to mind. Down the hallway behind the library was another room. The door to this room was locked. The room seemed not to have been visited in many years. Slowly I began to understand what this room was. It was the bedroom. Locked away behind its doors was intimacy. Abandonment. Oneness. Tenderness. Religious affection. Behind that door lay spiritual passion. I found myself retreating to the safety of the library, fearful of opening the door to passion. Passion frightened me—you get in trouble when you run the train by the caboose.

The spring of '97 taught me, however, that one tiny line in *The Four Spiritual Laws* doesn't ring true: "The train will run with or without the caboose." No. Not true. Not a chance! Edwards was right: "In religious matters the spring of [our] actions is very much religious affection." The coal car on the train of faith is passion.

THE DANGER OF HALF-BUILT CASTLES

Several miles down the river from my grandparents' cottage on the Saint Lawrence River is Heart Island. Nearly a century ago, a very wealthy man named Boldt bought the island for his wife and had it carved into the shape of a heart. This was only the beginning. Once the island was suitably carved, he began building a magnificent castle for his beloved wife. He imported marble from Italy, stone from Scotland, and art from the treasures of Europe. The towers and spires rose imperiously over the waters of the Saint Lawrence, and the castle looked as if it would rival those that dot the Rhine.

Then Mr. Boldt's wife died.

And so did his passion.

The workers were sent home. The Italian marble and Scottish stone were left on the docks. And the work on the castle ceased forever. Today you can still dock your boat at Heart Island and walk the lonely hallways of Mr. Boldt's half-built castle.

Many lives are half-built castles. Without passion, their dreams cannot be finished. With the death or absence of love, the drive to press on ebbs away, like the waters that swirl around the Scottish stone of Heart Island.

My ministry was in danger of becoming a half-built castle—a dream that began well, but might not be completed. Principled obedience was no longer enough. I needed passion. It was time to visit the bedroom, the place of passion, where dreams are conceived and castles are built.

> Passionate love for God leading to empowered, obedient living is the identifying mark of a word and power church.

Passionate love for God leading to empowered, obedient living is the identifying mark of a word and power church.

SEVEN HABITS OF HIGHLY PASSIONATE CHURCHES

Martin Luther once said that Christians were like drunks trying to ride a horse: We fall off one side and then fall off again on the other. (He had a way with words, didn't he?) How can we avoid falling off the horse on the side of fleshly emotion or on the side of dry, grim obedience? How can we create passionate churches where emotion is genuine and expressed in obedience? Passion is a gift of God. But there are spiritual habits we can practice in our churches that develop spiritual passion. Here are seven of them.

1. Highly passionate churches cast a vision for a passionate spirituality that moves beyond duty into delight. Biblical preaching is fundamentally about identity. Preaching answers the questions "Who is God?" and "Who am I?" Scripture uses several metaphors to describe our identity. We can place these metaphors on a continuum.

Clay
Sheep
Servant
Child
Friend
Lover

Most preaching focuses on our identity as sheep, servant, and child. Few sermons talk about our friendship with God. Hardly any unravel our identity as God's lover. Fellowship Church currently offers a course called "The Bride of Christ." It provides an in-depth look at what the Bible says about the church's identity as the bride and a careful explanation of what the bride-groom relationship looks like. The course is revolutionizing how people think about their relationship with God—and it is stirring a lot of passion.

2. Highly passionate churches create relational safe places where brokenness can be exposed and healed. James 5:16 tells us to confess our sins to one another and pray for one another that we may be healed. Nothing deadens spiritual passion more than carrying around secret sins. When secrets are shared in a place of love and truth, healing grace is released and so is passion.

It is no coincidence that the great commandment to love God is followed by the great commandment to love others. Loving God always happens in the midst of loving people. Spiritual passion is birthed amid loving relationships. We have often found that when spiritual passion is blocked in a person, God will use his gifts in the community to reveal what the blockage is. Passion is released as the barrier is removed through love, Scripture, and prayer.

3. Highly passionate churches develop an openness to kingdom breakthroughs. The paradox of the kingdom of God is that it is already here but it is not yet here. Jesus tells us to pray that the kingdom of heaven will break into this age. When the kingdom crashes into this world with divine power, our passion is stirred. These kingdom breakthroughs are the sparks that shower when two kingdoms collide with each other. And sparks like this ignite passion.

We pray for healing whenever we can. When God heals supernaturally, our hearts are set aflame with faith and hope. We recounted the story of Beth in chapter 6. Those friends and family believed God could heal her of this seemingly fatal meningitis. And he did.

We are also learning to see kingdom breakthroughs in the many ways God speaks to us and answers our prayers.

> If God says yes in answer to our prayers . . . most often those answers come to us by way of a messenger. That messenger may be an angel or a work of art, a prophet or a person we met for lunch, a Scripture or a song, a vision or a dream, a scene from nature or a night at the movies.[1]

I love watching people learn to hear the voice of God. All of life becomes sacred, every moment a potential "window of the soul," when you begin to live with the expectancy that God might show up anywhere and talk to you.

4. Highly passionate churches weave the rhythms of prayer throughout every aspect of church life. Prayer calls forth the presence of God. God's presence stirs passion. Fasting sweetens prayer. I spend one day a week in fasting and prayer, as do many people at Fellowship. A number of this group participated in extended fasts over the past year, including several forty-day fasts.

> All of life becomes sacred, every moment a potential "window of the soul," when you begin to live with the expectancy that God might show up anywhere and talk to you.

We have found that mobilizing and identifying our intercessors and bringing them more into the heart of our church life has fueled spiritual passion. As I write this book in a mountain cabin, various members of Fellowship's intercessory team have spent the day in a side room praying. Today, they are praying that God will use this chapter to release passion in you.

Prayer for one another kindles spiritual passion. Paul's pastoral prayer for his beloved Ephesians was basically a prayer for passion: "I pray that you ... may ... grasp how wide and long and high and deep is the love of Christ, and to know this love that surpasses knowledge— that you may be filled to the measure of all the fullness of God" (Eph. 3:17–19.) I am amazed at what happens in Fellowship Church when we gather around a friend for the sole purpose of stirring up spiritual passion. God reveals, he speaks, he leads, and he heals the twisted parts of the heart that rob passion. "You do not have," James reminds us, "because you do not ask God" (James 4:2). Why not ask for passion?

5. Highly passionate churches emphasize the supremacy of Christ in spiritual warfare. Who has more passion—a sleepy soldier cleaning a latrine in Fort Knox, Kentucky, three thousand miles away from the nearest battle, or a taut-muscled GI hanging out the door of a Huey chopper waiting to be dumped into a hot zone deep in the Vietnamese bush?

Many Christians have little passion for Jesus because they live in a peacetime mentality, not a wartime mentality. Passion grows when we realize that life is war and that the result will be heaven or hell.

Word and power churches believe in spiritual warfare. They believe in a real devil with real power who oversees real demons. And they believe in a real Jesus who is supremely victorious over every foe. A Western, rationalistic worldview that has no place for the demonic will deaden spiritual passion.

6. Highly passionate churches share stories. Storytelling calls forth passion much more than do carefully outlined propositions. We are rapidly becoming a people who think in narrative fashion, and our souls resonate with story.

Morgan, a pastor in a nearby town, joined the Pastors' Prayer Summit in Knoxville. On the final day the pastors were sharing praises of what God has done in our churches and community. Morgan, beaming, stood up and said, "I've got one. I was saved last night."

He was serious. Morgan had been religious for many years, but had never embraced Jesus in a personal way. His testimony was so powerful, I asked him to share his story at Fellowship the next Sunday. I had already prepared a sermon, so I asked Morgan to take only about five minutes. Morgan took the pulpit and told his story. When he finished, the presence of God hung over the room like evening mist over a mountain lake. Always perfectly in control, I bent over to an elder sitting next to me, and said, "What do I do now?"

"You'd be a fool if you preached after that. Give the folks a chance to respond."

I went to the platform and invited anyone who wanted to receive prayer to come forward. I will never forget what happened next. We had a response such as we have never seen before or since. Dozens of people streamed to the front, some sobbing uncontrollably. The sound of weeping, even wailing, filled the worship center as those God was touching wrestled with the sickness of sin in their souls.

The fruit from Morgan's story still grows. I know of at least one person who realized that she, too, was not a Christian and gave her heart to Christ. Many others experienced a deep inner renewal and hunger for the things of God. One man immediately began a fast that went on for days; he wanted nothing more than to be filled with God's presence.

All because of Morgan's story.

7. Highly passionate churches embrace the arts. Aleksandr Solzhenitsyn wrote, "Art can warm even a chilled and sunless soul to an exalted spiritual experience." Art can ignite spiritual passion.

There is a reason why God didn't build the temple like a national chain store. He called for his temple to be adorned with expensive, expressive works of sacred art. He knew that his followers, locked as we are in the prison of this fallen world, needed signs to point our gaze to heaven. He gave the arts to create within us the feelings of awe and reverence that awaken when one encounters the divine.

Our lust for the pragmatic and our ignorance of history cause us to miss one of the most significant ways God has met with his people throughout the ages—fine art. The churches of Europe, tragically absent now of the presence of God, were not always so. There was a day when the glorious design of these churches, with spires that ascended to the heavens and Bible stories spoken through the soft language of stained glass, called the faithful to know their God.

Willow Creek has done a tremendous job of reintroducing the church to drama. Dance ministries are emerging as well. I was speaking on spiritual passion at a conference for missionaries and hoping that the Lord would touch their hearts as well as their heads. We ended one session with a dance my wife performed to a song recorded by Pam Thumb, "Life Is Hard, But God Is Good."

The Holy Spirit used the song to touch places in the missionaries' hearts that my preaching had missed. One man said later that God spoke to him so powerfully in the dance that he ran from the room to a nearby field and stood there in the winter rain praying for the better part of an hour.

"A work of art introduces us to emotions which we have never cherished before," observed Abraham Heschel. "Great works produce rather than satisfy needs by giving the world fresh cravings."

⌁

True spirituality is passionate spirituality. Word and power churches encourage obedience by nurturing spiritual passion. We dare not ignore the caboose of our spiritual feelings. The train of spiritual living doesn't run well without it.

STUDY QUESTIONS _____

1. Are feelings an essential part of your relationship with God, or are you wary of their impact? How has your view of emotions changed during your spiritual journey?

2. What are the dangers of neglecting feelings, and what are the dangers of glorifying feelings? How do you strike a balance between the two?

3. Does your church express spiritual passion in obedience to the Word? How? Evaluate your church based on the Seven Habits of Highly Passionate Churches described in this chapter.

CHAPTER TEN

WORSHIP EVANGELISM

M y vote for the most significant evangelical leader in the last half of this century is Bill Hybels. Hybels, the dynamic founding pastor of the Willow Creek Community Church in Barrington, Illinois, has redefined the way the American church thinks about evangelicalism. Hybel's premise, communicated to thousands of church leaders each year through Willow Creek's leadership conferences, is simple: Believers and seekers have different needs. Therefore seeker services should be different from believer services.

Hybels, a compelling and passionate speaker, makes a strong case for this in his conferences by describing the dreadful experiences we have all had in bringing an unchurched friend to a traditional, believer-focused church service. Our friend squirms when the pastor asks him to stand up and "receive the special visitors' packet." Then the congregation stands for a rousing rendition of a great hit song from the 1860s. Our guest stands, too—a forlorn pelican isolated by his own ignorance of what the word *Ebenezer* means.

The coup de grace is the sermon, riddled with *Christianspeak*— those code words only we who are predestined, redeemed, and washed in the blood are anointed to know. On the way home, our friend thanks us for the invitation and then vows silently never to return to church again until his daughter's wedding, which, he now wonders, might come off better at a park after all.

Willow Creek responded to this need by offering two types of services. Believer services are offered on Wednesday and Thursday nights.

Seeker services are offered on Saturday evenings and on Sunday. Their believer services are an outstanding vehicle for discipleship; their leadership development and small-group ministry are unequaled. Those who criticize Willow Creek usually do so after visiting only a weekend seeker service. "That's not church," they huff. And in a sense they are right. But they miss the point. Willow Creek isn't trying to offer a church service on the weekend. It is targeting seekers, and there is a major difference from "church" in how that happens.

The seeker-service sermons are basic fare—"Christianity 101," Hybels calls them. Worship is brief and nonparticipatory because, Hybels feels, seekers are not used to singing. There is no altar call or prayer for people afterward. The seeker service is designed to be a "safe" place where irreligious people can be gently exposed to the claims of Christ without being turned away by the formal trappings of traditional church. The strategy has worked. Willow Creek has led thousands of seekers to Christ, and churches that have adopted their split format of seeker service/believer service have also been highly effective in evangelism.

Willow Creek wins the "sons of Issachar" award for being men and women "who understood the times and knew what Israel should do" (1 Chron. 12:32).

But the times have changed.

The world we are ministering to today is dramatically different from the world the church was speaking to in 1975 when Willow Creek's foundational premises were formed. Willow Creek was, is, and will remain effective in reaching baby boomers with the gospel. But another generation is coming behind the boomers, one called generation X. And they are as different from their boomer parents as boomers are from their own parents.

The differences between these two generations run far deeper than the token shifts in attitudes and taste (such as music styles, clothing fads, and favorite sayings) that have always marked the difference between generations.

A MASSIVE INTELLECTUAL REVOLUTION

A massive shift is taking place. Princeton theologian Diogenes Allen observes, "A massive intellectual revolution is taking place that is perhaps as great as that which marked off the modern world from the Middle Ages."[1] Culture watchers agree: "There has been a fundamental shift"² in our culture. The dividing line marking that shift is the one separating the boomer generation from generation X.

Sociologists and pundits have described the up-and-coming generation (technically defined as those born between 1961 and 1975) with numerous labels. "Generation X" is fitting for our purposes because the X represents a variable as yet unsolved. This generation has not yet figured out who they are, and the church has not yet figured out how to reach them.

And that matters. Because this generation represents where our culture is headed. We need to develop our ministry strategies by looking ahead and assessing the needs of the next generation instead of looking back to the needs of 1975.

> The times demand that we create word and power churches that both edify the believer *and* evangelize the seeker *at the same time.*

I do not believe that Hybel's premise is valid in reaching the new generation. It is no longer necessary to have *either* a worship service for believers *or* an evangelistic service for seekers. The times demand that we embrace the genius of the AND by creating word and power churches that both edify the believer *and* evangelize the seeker *at the same time.*

Xers are different from boomers in two very significant ways. (Although I tend to shun categorization, I know of no more user-friendly way to look at this massive cultural shift than by labeling these two generations and treating them with the inevitable over-simplification that regrettably results. Forgive me.)

First, boomers typically hear the gospel the best when it is communicated in terms of facts, principles, or laws. Xers think differently about truth, and many no longer even believe in truth. They are more likely to respond to the gospel when it is communicated as a story that intersects with their own story.

Second, boomers normally make decisions on the basis of reason. Xers, because of their skepticism toward the idea of truth (whose truth is true?), are more prone to make decisions on the basis of experience.

TELL ME A STORY

Why do I love *The Four Spiritual Laws?* Because I am a baby boomer. I love laws, principles, reasons that I can list out, weigh the pros and cons of, and then judge. I'm like Joe Friday in the old *Drag-net* TV show—"Just the facts, ma'am. Just give me the facts." I became deeply committed to my faith in college because it seemed to have the most coherent presentation of truths. The facts seemed to add up the best in Christianity.

Evangelism, naturally, was presenting the facts.

We shared those beloved Four Laws. We gave away truckloads of Josh McDowell's book *Evidence That Demands a Verdict*. We brought in professors who would argue about proofs for the Resurrection or debate other professors. We wanted to show that Christianity is *true*.

Christianity *is* true. The only problem is, Xers no longer believe in truth.

Walter Truett Anderson tells a joke to describe the different ways people think about truth:

> Three umpires were having a Coke after a baseball game. One says, "There's balls and there's strikes and I call 'em the way they are."
>
> Another responds, "There's balls and there's strikes and I call 'em the way I see 'em."
>
> The third umpire says, "There's balls and there's strikes and they ain't nothin' until I call 'em."[3]

Many people who live on this side of the great massive intellectual shift described by Professor Allen see truth the same way the third umpire does—truth isn't truth until I decide it is. For the past four hundred years, most people have felt pretty good about truth. Think hard enough and ultimately you'll get where you need to go. Not everyone believed that truth was found in Jesus, but almost everyone believed in some sort of absolute truth that spread like an invisible umbrella over us all, protecting our lives and our culture.

Not anymore. The mantra today is pluralism. It now sounds arrogant to say, "I know the truth." The greatest virtue is tolerating opposing truth claims rather than defending your own.

But Jesus is the Truth! Is there no hope? How can we tell the truth to a new culture that no longer even believes in truth?

The same way Jesus did. By telling stories.

Your neighbor may not believe in truth. But his heart longs to be a part of a larger story. Leighton Ford has given his life to discovering how to share the gospel with a shifting culture. The evangelist had traveled the world at the side of Billy Graham, preaching to hundreds of thousands of people. The death of Ford's son, Sandy, changed the focus of his life and ministry. Dr. Ford became an avid student of the youth culture. He noticed that the old ways of evangelism didn't seem to reach them anymore. He talked with the next generation about who they are, where they want to go, and what they believe. He ransacked the libraries and visited with scholars to see what the philosophers and theologians were saying about the changing face of America's mission field. The fruit of this search is Dr. Ford's landmark book *The Power of Story*. His thesis is that "narrative evangelism is an evangelism for the times we live in. . . . I am convinced there is a longing to hear the Story of an accessible, approachable, loving God."[4] The evangelist defines effective evangelism as showing people how their stories intersect with his Story.

The average age of Fellowship's congregation is thirty-one. This does not make me an expert on speaking to generation X. But I have noticed that the younger members of the church are not clamoring for facts and proofs and classic apologetics the way my generation did. They yearn instead to weave their life story within a larger script—a sacred romance in which God is both author and lover. They want someone to tell them a story, an epic, that speaks to life's quests and longings.

Douglas Coupland's novel *Generation X* is a disturbing chronicle of three young people who find themselves living in a terrifying world where truth has died. Narrated with chilling detachment by a twenty-seven-year-old Palm Springs bartender named Andy, the story winds through the wasteland of popular culture, offering painful insights and very little hope. Andy, Claire, and Dag have two pleasures in life: being together and telling bedtime stories. The trio, who live in the same lower-income condo complex, put on their pajamas, crawl up onto a bed, and spend the evening spinning "tales for an accelerated culture."

> Younger church members yearn to weave their life story within a larger script—a sacred romance in which God is both author and lover.

The theme of storytelling is woven throughout the novel. At one point Claire says, "Either our lives become stories, or there's just no way to get through them."

Agreeing, Andy confesses to his readers, "We know that this is why the three of us left our lives behind us and came to the desert— to tell stories and to make our own lives worthwhile tales in the process."[5]

Andy never reaches the goal that led him to the desert. No one in the novel ever makes peace with his or her own story. This should not surprise us. Storytelling alone cannot speak to the deeper longings of our souls. It is only when we connect our stories with the Story that life begins to make sense.

We serve a talking God, and when he talks he tells love stories. He tells a story about a loving father who searches for his lost and rebellious children. He tells a story about a groom pursuing a wayward bride. He tells a story about a shepherd looking for lost sheep. He tells a story about a widow searching for a lost coin.

The Bible is a love story, a divine romance filled with pursuit, betrayal, conquest, and intrigue. It begins with a divorce and ends with a marriage. His Son died to tell this story. Our neighbors are dying to hear it.

When men and women heard the gospel best through propositions and facts, it made sense to share those facts, keeping in mind that seekers need one set of facts, saints another. The rules change, however, when your congregation is seeking not facts but a Story. The biblical story touches seeker and saint alike.

Frederick Dale Bruner has written one of the century's best commentaries on the gospel of Matthew. He learned something about the power of story in writing it.

> After several years of struggling to find the right text for teaching Christian doctrine in Asia, something good happened in the Sunday school class at our barrio church . . . where some of the seminary students attended. I was teaching the parables of Matthew 13 where Jesus explains the meaning of the kingdom of God. The same students whose eyes glazed over when I taught the doctrine of God in the seminary's Christian doctrine class now seemed alive with interest when they heard Jesus teach the kingdom of God in [stories].[6]

My preaching has changed considerably over the past decade. My early sermons were primarily concerned with communicating propositions about God. This was consistent with my belief that loving God was primarily understanding his principles and obeying them. Today my preaching remains expositional, but my broader goal is placing those truths in the context of a larger story. Narrative books, of course, are the easiest Bible texts to tell the story from. Yet even the most tightly argued doctrinal passages tell a story as well. The doctrine of adoption is the story of God's ravishing, selecting love. The doctrine of eternal judgment is the story of love and the freedom to reject it. The doctrine of sin is the story of relationship and betrayal.

> Word and power churches have a Story to tell more than they have facts to tell.

Storytelling is not the lazy habit of filling sermons with trivial anecdotes (like "I was at the barber the other day and ...."). Preaching that speaks to a culture's longing for story addresses the questions of meaning, purpose, and fulfillment that both seekers and believers are asking. Preaching that is supplemented with dance, drama, or testimony is even more effective at capturing the heart of a story-starved generation.

Many more unchurched people attend our services now than in the church's early days. Yet even believers tell me their lives change more under this kind of preaching than by the way I preached before.

Word and power churches have a Story to tell more than they have facts to tell. Biblical preaching and Scripture study that penetrate the next generation will call God's people to consider a new script for their lives, a script authored by a loving Father and written in the blood of his Son.

CLEAN POWER

A man I will call Bill tossed his navy blazer on a paper-covered desk and poured his lanky frame into an overstuffed chair, motioning for me to sit across from him. He looked tired from the pressures of running the large organization surrounding him. And he was ready to talk.

Bill is a deeply spiritual man who rejected the conservative (he would say "fundamentalist") Christianity of his youth as he gathered graduate degrees in religion during the seventies. His life is consumed with spiritual pursuit. He is a man who truly wants to know God.

"So," he began, "tell me something."

I wasn't ready for the question that came next.

"Do you speak in tongues?"

What followed was a fascinating discussion about God and how one knows him. Bill's spiritual journey was driven by a quest for a God he could experience.

"Why did you leave your church?" I asked Bill as our time drew to a close.

"Because I wanted to worship a God who would talk to me. And I didn't find him there."

Bill's journey reflects the spirit of the coming age more than the one that is passing away. He is not weighing competing worldviews and trying on the one that seems the most reasonable. He is looking for a God who will touch him.

Most people who have left the modern era behind no longer believe there is one true God. Theological pluralism has won the day, and many of our neighbors—especially if they are under thirty-five—shop for their god in a marketplace crammed full of competing deities. Sociologist Peter Berger sees pluralism as one of the dominant forces shaping our culture, which means "the man on the street is confronted with a wide variety of religious [options] that compete for his allegiance."[7]

How will he choose?

He will choose the God he can experience—the God who proves by his power his greatness over all other gods. Churches that reach people like my friend Bill will do so by creating environments where the presence of God is so real he cannot be denied. Bill must meet the God who talks.

The church has been there before.

Yale historian Ramsay MacMullen notes in his classic work *Christianizing the Roman Empire* that one reason for the gospel's dramatic progress in a pagan world with dozens of would-be gods was the supernatural works of power that confirmed the message. "Driving all competition from the field head on was crucial," MacMullen writes. "The world, after all, held many dozens and hundreds of gods. Choice was open to everybody. It could be only a most exceptional force that would actually displace alternatives and compel allegiance. . . . [These demonstrations] were the chief instrument of conversion."[8]

The Willow Creek model assumes that seekers will be more prone to make decisions for Christ in an environment where they are safely detached from what is happening on stage and where they are not exposed to prolonged worship, prophetic ministry, prayer for healing, and other practices that might take place in a believers' service. This assumption generally holds true for the baby boomer audience. Boomers often do need a safe place to process the gospel message and quietly make their decision.

This assumption does not hold true, however, with the next generation. Churches that reach Xers will be saturated with the power and presence of God. When I interview our new members and ask them why they have come to Fellowship, the overwhelming answer is "the worship." This is especially true with unchurched people and people under thirty-five. "I meet God in the worship," they say. "I never knew you could actually experience God. I just thought you could learn about him." Powerful worship that invites the presence of God draws seekers rather than repels them. Genuine worship is evangelistic.

D. Martyn Lloyd-Jones's biographer tells the story of a well-known London spiritist who was converted to Christ after attending Westminster Chapel. "The moment I entered your chapel and sat down on a seat amongst the people, I was conscious of a supernatural power," the woman recalled. "I was conscious of the same sort of supernatural power as I was accustomed to in our spiritist meetings, but there was one big difference; I had the feeling that the power in your chapel was a clean power."[9]

Word and power churches invite God's "clean" power through worship. They invite his power through prayer-saturated preaching. They invite his power by a prophetic word. They invite his power by praying for the emotionally and spiritually wounded.

The apostle Paul tells us that revealing God's presence to the lost is one purpose of the power gifts. "If an unbeliever . . . comes in while everybody is prophesying, he will be convinced by all that he is a sinner . . . , and the secrets of his heart will be laid bare. So he will fall down and worship God, exclaiming, 'God is really among you!'" (1 Cor. 14:24–25).

My two sisters-in-law are generation Xers who came to Christ in their late teens. My wife and I had witnessed to them for several years and hopefully planted the seed of the gospel in their hearts.

Yet it was the worship of the Anaheim Vineyard Church that ultimately drew them into the kingdom. They *heard about* God from us. They *met* God in the worship.

Harvard theologian Harvey Cox became famous thirty years ago by proclaiming the imminent death of religion in the coming "postreligious age." Now he sees things quite differently. His recent book *Fire From Heaven* is about Pentecostalism and its vitality in a world that longs to encounter God. Cox recalls attending a Pentecostal rally during his freshman year of college. He and another young intellectual went "to see the show." Cox remembers,

> We walked to his trolley stop [afterwards] without saying anything, and as he climbed on board I just said, "Really something, eh, Bill?"
>
> "Yeah," he answered, still staring straight ahead as the trolley pulled away. I could sense that although we had come mainly out of curiosity, maybe even to be entertained, we had found ourselves in the presence of something that was more than we expected.[10]

The collapse of truth has not killed our neighbors' hunger for God. It has unleashed it. We live in a day of intense spiritual longing. Why else would five and a half million pilgrims a year visit the shrine of Lourdes in France, hoping for a miracle? Someone asked the priest why they came. He replied, "Perhaps people find religious life too monotonous and want something more intense, more festive, more emotional. Perhaps the form our religion has taken does not respond to people's needs."

> The collapse of truth has not killed our neighbors' hunger for God. It has unleashed it.

When Fellowship Church first began to learn about the power gifts six years ago, I responded with a sense of resigned obedience. "Lord, if you really want us to pray for people in the services, or learn about the prophetic, or even allow folks to receive a prayer language, we will, because that's what your Word says. It'll probably slow down our growth, though. But you are sovereign. I'll leave the growth to you."

The church has quadrupled in size since I prayed that prayer. I believe we have stumbled onto a "form of religion that responds to people's needs."

The great German theologian Rudolf Otto contends that while true religion begins with a rational knowledge of God, it must never end there. The end of true worship, he says, is a sense of "mystical awe" in God's presence. Sometimes, he continues, "this feeling or consciousness of the 'wholly other' will . . . be indirectly aroused by means of . . . extraordinary phenomena or astonishing occurrences . . . among men."[11]

Word and power churches lead people into divine encounter with the one who is Wholly Other. That's why they come back.

NEW DAYS, NEW PARADIGMS

God is blending together the strengths of the evangelical and charismatic traditions to equip us to speak to the next generation. Our mission field is changing. The neighbor we must reach today is vastly different from the neighbor we tried to reach yesterday. She longs to hear a love story; she's looking for a God she can experience. She will find both in the word and power church.

A generation ago, it made sense to split up the church's ministry and offer one service for seekers and one service for believers. That model will be useful as long as the past generation still needs to hear the gospel.

Churches that want to reach the next generation, however, will find that saints and seekers are looking for the same thing: A Story that makes sense out of life written by a God they can feel.

STUDY QUESTIONS

1. Are you a boomer or an Xer or of another generation? Do the generalizations about your group ring true? How does your outlook impact the way you relate with others?

2. What types of people primarily compose your church: boomers or Xers? How does this affect the way you worship?

3. Does your church practice "worship evangelism"? In other words, is God's presence made known through your worship? How can you develop this more?

CHAPTER ELEVEN

POWER AND PAIN

C hristy's mother handed me a folded sheet of notebook paper when I greeted her that Saturday outside her daughter's room in the hallway of Children's Hospital.

"These are some of Christy's questions," she said, tears glistening in her tired eyes. "I'm having a hard time answering them."

I slowly unfolded the paper. It looked at first glance like a list of test questions any fourteen-year-old might take down off the board to prepare for tomorrow's social studies exam. But these questions were of a different kind. And this was a different kind of exam.

This was Christy's first question: *Why does God let fourteen-year-old girls die from leukemia?*

Christy was losing a two-year battle with cancer. She was dying, and she knew it. Several hours after I read this paper, Christy slipped into a coma. Dozens of Christy's friends and her family arrived on the fifth floor of the hospital to make one final assault on death. Weary, weeping loved ones knelt in hallways, in stairwells, and in the waiting room, offering up desperate prayers mingled with hope and anger, fear and faith. Hundreds prayed and fasted around the clock throughout the city. Christy's elders anointed her with oil, laid hands on her, and prayed. Shell-shocked teachers and students at her Christian school called off classes, held onto one another, and prayed for a miracle.

Then Christy died.

A week later, I was chopping wood in my backyard when the phone rang. It was Children's Hospital. Could I please come down immediately? A routine ultrasound had discovered a three-pound cancerous tumor on my daughter Bryden's kidney. Dr. Pace, Christy's doctor, would see us in an hour.

Now we, too, had joined the strange fraternity of families battling children's cancer. Would the final chapter for us be the same as theirs?

Our church, still grieving and exhausted, now rallied around us. Prayers went up through the night and around the world. The elders came and anointed Bryden with oil and prayed over her. The hallways of Children's Hospital once again were rendered impassable by our friends as they stormed heaven with prayer for my daughter's healing.

This time, God's answer was *yes*.

Today, three and a half years later, Bryden is free of cancer.

THE PROBLEM WITH FORMULAS

Whenever I hear formulaic approaches to God's healing ("God always . . . ," "God never . . . ," "If you . . . he will . . ."), I remember those long hours in Children's Hospital—first as a pastor, then as a parent. Pain, especially the pain of seeing children suffer, defies formulas. Did we have "more faith" than Christy's parents? No. Their faith and witness during their ordeal was heroic and humbling. Did we have "more" or "better" prayers? No way. If divine healing takes "more" and "better" prayers than those offered for Christy, then God is deaf and we are all dead men walking.

God simply refuses to submit to The Way We Think God Should Do Things.

God is God. He does what he chooses. The unsettling, maddening reality about divine healing is this: Sometimes God heals, sometimes he doesn't, and he never bothers to tell us why.

Nowhere is it more important for us to embrace the genius of the AND than in our understanding of healing and suffering, because both are part of kingdom life.

Historically the church has refused to live in a biblical tension about God's healing ministry. Some churches never pray for healing. Some believe healing is a Christian's divine right. The truth, as it usually is, is somewhere in the middle. We are the clay,

> God simply refuses to submit to The Way We Think God Should Do Things.

God the potter. Who are we to tell the potter how to shape us? Word and power churches pray fervently for healing, and they comfort those who remain afflicted. They have a place in their theology, and in their hearts, for Christy's family and for Bryden's family, for heaven's yeses and heaven's nos.

HEALING MINISTRY IN THE LOCAL CHURCH

Churches that do not pray for the sick are ignoring a clear biblical command. James commands,

> Is anyone of you sick? He should call the elders of the church to pray for him and anoint him with oil in the name of the Lord. And the prayer offered in faith will make the sick person well; the Lord will raise him up. If he has sinned, he will be forgiven. Therefore confess your sins to each other and pray for each other so that you may be healed. The prayer of a righteous man is powerful and effective (James 5:14–16).

How many of our churches are indicted by Ezekiel's prophecy against poor shepherds? "Woe to the shepherds . . . who only take care of themselves. . . . You have not strengthened the weak or healed the sick or bound up the injured" (Ezek. 34:2, 4).

Twelve years ago I did not see praying for the sick as part of the shepherds' job. When I and the elders did pray together, it was somewhat reluctantly and usually at the end of a long meeting. Several years ago a single mother with a life-threatening illness called the elders for prayer. I found myself wincing—we already had a full agenda. I scheduled a prayer time for her anyway. We prayed earnestly, but without a lot of energy and focus because we had already put in a full day.

This woman told me later that our half-hearted prayer for her was devastating and even caused her to doubt God's love for her. She was a new believer, yet she knew that James 5 told her to seek prayer for her illness. Did we believe in James 5, she wondered? I was crushed.

We have since repented of our failure to obey James 5:14–16, which is a failure to shepherd the flock. We believe, on the basis of James' command, that prayer for the sick is one of the primary ways we are to shepherd our flock.

SOMETIMES THE ANSWER IS NO

We also believe that God often says no when we ask him to heal. Even the mighty apostles did not see every healing prayer answered with a dramatic yes. Paul left Trophimus sick in Miletus (2 Tim. 4:20). Paul told Timothy to take some wine for his stomach problems and frequent illnesses (1 Tim. 5:23). Even Paul himself appears not to have been supernaturally healed from the ailment he alludes to in his letter to the Galatians (Gal. 4:13–14.)

Suffering is an inevitable part of life on a fallen planet. Our broken world is described as "groaning" and in "bondage to decay" (Rom. 8:22, 21). Jesus did not heal every ailing person he encountered, and neither will we.

Typically, when someone asks me how my daughter is doing, I reply, "By God's grace, she is doing well." I almost wrote those words into my earlier description of Bryden's recovery. Then I stopped and asked, "Where was God's grace when Christy died?" Many of us would think, "Not much grace there. The whole ordeal sounds pretty graceless."

Christy's parents see it differently. Their daughter's absence still hangs over their life like a cloudy sky. Yet they will tell you that they met God's grace in Christy's death. They met his love. They met his kindness. Could it be that Christy died "by God's grace" just as Bryden lived by it? Could it be that God is sovereign and that his grace is displayed in death and in life, in agony and in healing?

The desk where I am writing is surrounded by books on healing. Each author seems pushed onward by some strange force to unravel the mysteries of suffering and healing. One takes aim at the classic evangelical belief that God uses suffering to sanctify us. "With sickness viewed as a possible benefit to spiritual transformation," he reasons, "praying for healing becomes less frequent."[1] Others painstakingly try to distinguish the source of sickness—is it Satan, or is it God? Does God "permit" and Satan "cause"? Some books champion healing as an aid to evangelism: God will draw attention to himself as he heals the sick and displays his compassion and power to a fallen world. Others vigorously refute such a claim and reply that there is no greater symbol of God's power than a Christian enduring suffering with humility, dignity, and peace.

My take on the matter is that each of these books is right. And each of them is wrong.

God is glorified when he heals. God is glorified when he ennobles us to suffer with hope and dignity. God's compassion extends to us when he lifts us out of our pain. God's compassion extends to us when he holds our hand and walks through our pain with us. God bears witness to a hurting world with the conspicuous power of signs and wonders. God bears witness to a hurting world with the quiet power of a holy life. God draws us toward holiness both when he heals us and when he allows us to share the fellowship of his sufferings.

God uses pain *and* power to glorify his name and make us more like him.

Word and power churches aren't afraid of living in this paradox. After all, this is the paradox of the "already but not yet" kingdom of God. The kingdom both *is* here and *is not* here. Hence there will be power and there will be pain. Both are by God's grace.

> God uses pain *and* power to glorify his name and make us more like him.

Tucked away in the basement of Children's Hospital is a small interdenominational chapel (go toward Radiology and take a left). I spent many hours there during Bryden's stay. Sometimes I prayed for healing. Sometimes, more often I think, I prayed in the spirit of Philippians 3:10, that I would "know Christ and the power of his resurrection and the fellowship of sharing in his sufferings." Both prayers were answered. Bryden was healed; the cancer seems to be gone. Yet Bryden also suffered; her hair fell out from the chemotherapy on Christmas Eve, she threw up and shivered, and she had to have blood transfusions.

We met God's grace in the healing: he spared our daughter's life. We met God's grace in the suffering: he suffered with us and never let us go.

Four Healing Myths

Everyone has a horror story about the healing ministry. We prayed recently for a young mother who was about to have her fourth brain surgery. "We had to leave our church to get prayed for," she said softly, wiping mascara off her cheeks. "They just didn't do that there."

Another time a number of us prayed for a woman with cancer. Some in the group sensed that God was going to give her a dramatic healing and told her that. Her hopes were raised. When the cancer remained, her hopes were dashed. At Fellowship we have made our share of mistakes in trying to become a church that fervently prays for the sick but also submits to what God might do through suffering. Most of the time mistakes in a healing ministry are a result of inexperience. We evangelicals are pretty new at this!

Some healing ministry, however, wounds rather than heals because it is based on bad doctrine. There are four common myths that can hinder a healing ministry.

Myth 1: "If only you have enough faith, you will be healed." Most doctrinal errors include some biblical truth, and this error is no exception. Jesus said to the woman who was healed of internal bleeding that had gone on for twelve years, "Take heart, daughter, your faith has healed you" (Matt. 9:22). And who will deny James' promise that "the prayer offered in faith" will make a sick person well?

Yet this is not the whole story. Jesus heals some who give no evidence of faith (the blind man in John 9:1–5, for example). Paul repeatedly prayed with faith for God to take the "thorn" of suffering from him, and God said no (2 Cor. 12:7–9). These texts rule out any magic formulas.

Faith *does* please God and *does* draw forth his presence, blessing, and grace. But remember, *God's presence, blessing, and grace will look different in different lives*. God honored Christy's parents' faith by walking with them through the valley of the shadow of death rather than by healing. What we can be sure of is that faith-based praying summons the presence of God. What God will do when he is present is up to him. "Our God is in heaven; he does whatever pleases him" (Ps. 115:3).

Healing ministry becomes hurtful when the ones who are sick believe they are ultimately responsible for their own healing by having to stir up the right amount of faith.

Myth 2: "If you really trust in God to heal, you will not take your medicine." The Trojan horse of the "either-or" fallacy slips into camp by positing two types of healing against one another. The myth suggests that supernatural healing is of God and medical healing is not. Push this line of thinking to its logical conclusion and here is where you end up: Doctors are for those with weak faith; strong believers who really trust God pray and don't need medical help.

But isn't all healing God's work? Are the pharmaceutical companies responsible for the healing that occurs from their drugs, or do we give God the glory for these healings, too? Shouldn't we thank and praise God for penicillin and polio vaccines, for ultrasounds and chemotherapy?

Bryden would not be alive today if she had not received chemotherapy treatments. Prayer helped her endure the chemotherapy and enhanced its effectiveness. God used both means to heal.

Physicians should be seen as allies in healing, not adversaries. One woman at Fellowship takes weekly shots to fight off a life-threatening nervous disorder. She has received extensive healing prayer and has seen remarkable improvement. When she sensed it was time to back off from her shots, she told this to her Christian doctor. He prayed for her and agreed to her plan, and together they are monitoring her progress.

Myth 3: "True healing must be dramatic and instantaneous or it isn't real." Healing ministries are often set back by the false demand that they be exactly like the healing ministry of Jesus and the apostles. Healings that are partial or gradual in nature are dismissed as false because "that's not like they did it in the book of Acts."

I am not aware of any healing ministry in the history of the church that rivals in power and drama the healing ministry of the apostles. There was something unique and foundational about their ministry (Eph. 2:20). The often-heard charge is true: Nobody does healing today like the apostle Paul. But must we conclude from that that God is done with his healing ministry?

No one preaches as Paul did, but we still preach. No one evangelizes as Peter did, but we still evangelize. No one heals as the apostles did, but we can still pray for healing.

Sometimes we experience dramatic healings. But most of the time God touches people gradually and partially. We still give God glory for this and see these infusions of heavenly power as tokens of the age to come, evidences of the kingdom breaking through into this age.

I fell out of a boat while attending a Fourth of July party and landed on a submerged dock, badly bruising my lower back. (My hosts were so compassionate that at the end of our evening together I was given the award for "preacher conducting the best self-baptism.") Several days later, the soreness grew worse. I asked the prayer team who were with me that day to pray for my back. They prayed simple prayers inviting God to heal. When they finished praying, the pain was not gone, but it had significantly lessened.

Was this an apostolic style "sign and wonder"? Probably not. But my back felt a lot better, and I thank God for that.

We are discovering that soaking a person in prayer over a season of weeks and months often advances their healing significantly. We don't despise the day of small things. You're not Peter, and I'm not Paul. Let us be thankful we have a God who still heals and be thankful for what does happen when we pray.

Myth 4: "Healing ministry is individuals praying over the sick." When most people think of healing ministry, they think of "faith healers"—certain people with the gift of healing who make a living going from town to town praying for people. (Evangelicals typically are suspicious of most itinerant healers.)

The Scriptures, however, don't describe healing ministry as centered in an individual. James calls the elders to pray and urges the congregation to pray for one another. Paul tells the Corinthians that the Spirit gives "gifts of healing" (1 Cor. 12:9) for the body to share among them. The plural use suggests that this is not a permanent gift that resides in a certain person, but that each healing is a gift, given by the Spirit, to meet a need in the body. Anyone can pray for healing, and anyone can ask for "gifts of healing" to be given during prayer for the sick.

Some people do seem more effective than others in praying for the ill, and we can be thankful for them. Yet it is not helpful or biblical to set apart some as "healers." This practice merely reinforces the myth that only certain people can pray for healing, when in fact this is every believer's privilege. The "healer" myth also communicates that the only times God heals are in large, Pentecostal-style healing meetings. I believe God does heal in these meetings, but that is not the only place God heals. He heals wherever

> Let us be thankful we have a God who still heals and be thankful for what does happen when we pray.

God's people gather to pray over a hurting friend. At Fellowship we are trying to weave healing ministry into the normal rhythms of our life together.

THREE PRINCIPLES FOR EFFECTIVE HEALING PRAYER

How can a word and power church fervently pray for the sick without hurting those who are not healed? The following three principles are an attempt to start us down the right path.

Principle 1: Effective healing prayer is listening prayer. Don't immediately pray for healing for everyone who asks for healing. The key to answered prayer is discovering God's will and praying it. Why pray for healing if that isn't what the Father intends for a person's life?

As we have noted, Jesus did not heal everyone who was sick. He healed those whom the Father was choosing to heal. The ancient world's equivalent to a hospital was the healing pool. There dozens of the sick and lame gathered in the hopes that the pool's "magical" waters would heal them.

Jesus approached one of these pools on a trip to Jerusalem. The gospel of John tells us that a "great number" of sick people lay beside the pool. Jesus addressed only one man, a paralytic who had been an invalid for thirty-eight years. "Pick up your mat and walk," Jesus commanded him. And the man did (John 5:1–15).

> Effective healing prayer begins by listening to the voice of God.

Significantly, Jesus did not heal anyone else of the "great number" of sick people who were at the pool that day. Why did he single out this man? "I tell you the truth," Jesus said a few hours after the healing, "the Son can do nothing by himself; he can do only what he sees his Father doing, because whatever the Father does the Son also does" (John 5:19).

Jesus healed the man where the Father was already working. The Son joined the Father where the Father was already at work. Even Jesus did not initiate divine healing ("How about this one, Father? He has great faith."). Rather, Jesus waited upon his Father to show him whom he was to heal. Can we do anything less when we are ministering to the sick and wounded?

Effective healing prayer begins by listening to the voice of God. Paul's description of body ministry in 1 Corinthians 12:7–11 shows how the healing gifts are released along with the speaking gifts.

Now to each one the manifestation of the Spirit is given for the common good. To one there is given through the Spirit the message of wisdom, to another the message of knowledge by means of the same Spirit, to another faith by the same Spirit, to another gifts of healing by that one Spirit, to another miraculous powers, to another prophecy, to another distinguishing between spirits, to another speaking in different kinds of tongues, and to still another the interpretation of tongues. All these are the work of one and the same Spirit, and he gives them to each one, just as he determines.

Notice how the speaking gifts are given along with the gifts of healing. Bible teachers disagree about the exact nature of some of these gifts. We see them under the broad heading of the prophetic—they are all different ways the talking God reveals his will and ways. Healing prayer without listening prayer is incomplete prayer. These gifts help us discern what the Father is doing in the person's life.

James tells us to confess our sins to one another in the midst of healing prayer. Fellowship starts healing prayer times by reading James 5:14–18 and gently asking the person requesting prayer if God has used the sickness to reveal any area of sin in his or her life. Sin, of course, is not the cause of all sickness, but a surprising amount of physical pain has spiritual and emotional roots. This is especially true where there is bitterness.

In prayer teams we have spent the whole prayer time dealing with bitterness and then find at the end of the session that the physical symptom of illness is gone. Once we have allowed the person receiving prayer to confess any known sin, we sit quietly before the Lord and ask him to show us how to pray. Sometimes we may sit for as long as fifteen minutes before someone senses a direction in prayer. We may read a passage of Scripture, ask a question, or pray for guidance. Gradually a prayer strategy is discerned. Generally we are led to pray in one of three ways: for healing, for the person's strength amid suffering, and, occasionally, as a channel for God's speaking to the person through the sickness.

Principle 2: The richer the relationships, the greater the healing. I know people who have been radically transformed of both physical and emotional problems while standing in a huge crowd and being prayed for by a speaker who had never met them.

More often that not, however, effective healing prayer occurs where there are safe, authentic relationships. We have seen that faith invites the presence of God; faith is stirred when we are with those we know and love. We have also seen that confession invites God's healing touch; this, too, is more natural in a safe relational environment.

Healing prayer is often self-disclosing prayer. Body and soul are much more closely woven together than we sometimes realize. Prayer for the body very frequently becomes prayer for the soul as well. In dealing with a physical wound, the Spirit may gently open emotional wounds and cleanse them first. He surfaces painful memories and past brokenness that have been covered over but not healed. The healing process can be traumatic to the person receiving prayer. This trauma is lessened when those praying are friends who have already earned the trust of the hurting person.

> Healing prayer is more the beginning of a journey than the end of a problem.

Spiritual growth is a process best experienced when life is shared with others. Healing prayer is more the beginning of a journey than the end of a problem. Healing prayer releases us to press on in our spiritual pilgrimage. Prayer times often reveal character areas that need to be shored up by Scripture study, discipline, and mutual accountability. It is very important not to abandon people after the Spirit has powerfully engaged them. Loving relationships help people move beyond their healing and establish the effective spiritual habits that will protect them from soul injury in the future.

Principle 3: Nos and yeses both come from a good God. When God does not grant a gift of healing in response to our prayers, many feel like failures and give up, blaming themselves, or the friend being prayed for, or worse, the God who didn't answer.

This kind of thinking is rooted in the myth that God wants to heal everyone. The truth is, God doesn't want to heal everybody. If he did, everybody around the pool in Jerusalem would have been healed that day when Jesus passed by.

When we fervently pray for a sick friend and the answer from heaven seems to be a clear "No, it is not in my plan to heal him at this time," we should then change our prayer strategy. Paul changed his after the Lord refused to take away the thorn in his flesh. "Three times I pleaded with the Lord to take it away from me. But he said to me, 'My grace is sufficient for you, for my power is made perfect in weakness'" (2 Cor. 12:8–9).

Paul did not pout, doubt his faith, or question God's goodness when he was not healed. God spoke to him and told him that his will was for Paul to experience grace and power in the midst of suffering. We who live in the tension between the already and the not yet will often find ourselves in the same place as Paul, longing for a "yes" and hearing instead a "no." If we communicate that there has been failure when we don't get what we ask for, we will crush the spirit or the faith of the person we are praying for. Instead, we need to understand—and communicate—that the Father is simply doing something else and we need to cooperate with that.

Paul's very words were, "He said to me." God wants to speak to us, too. He wants to show us why our prayers are not being answered. He wants to redirect our prayers and mingle them with his own. When our prayers for healing are not answered, we must listen to the voice of God. What is the Father doing? Should we press on and persevere? Should we change the focus of our prayers?

Why is it that we stop praying passionately for people when there appears to be no divine healing? Isn't it equally as valuable to pray for people in the middle of their suffering? Churches that celebrate divine healing from suffering must also celebrate divine endurance in suffering.

A GRIEF OBSERVED

C. S. Lewis wrote two books on pain. The first one, *The Problem of Pain,* is a brilliant academic discussion of one of philosophy's greatest questions. The second, *A Grief Observed,* is a brutally honest tour through the wasteland of Lewis's heart after his wife Joy died. Lewis takes us to hell and back again with riveting candor and lets us wander with him as his soul finds its way back home.

The first book is the work of a scholar.

The second book is the work of a man who was getting to know his God.

Pain has a way of changing people that way.

God's greatest goal for us is that we might know him. He orders all of life to guide us into a deeper relationship with him. He may spare us pain so that we might know the mercy of his favor. He may walk with us through pain so that we might know the fellowship of his sufferings. His goal in both is the same: our knowing him.

Lewis writes in *The Problem of Pain* that pain is God's megaphone used to rouse a deaf world. Word and power churches believe that. They see healing as a megaphone, too.

STUDY QUESTIONS

1. Have you ever sincerely prayed for healing for yourself or others? How did God respond?

2. Discuss how your church has been influenced by the five myths about healing. How can you promote truth in your church?

3. Discuss the three principles for effective healing. How evident are those principles in your church?

CHAPTER TWELVE

DAILY FILLINGS AND DEEPER WORKS

I will never forget the first time I heard Bill Bright speak. It was at the 1981 Campus Crusade Christmas Conference in Chicago. His theme: the "exciting adventure of the Spirit-filled life." Dr. Bright talked about the vital importance of living each day filled with the power of the Holy Spirit. He taught us to "breathe spiritually" each day, exhaling our sin and self-reliance, inhaling the empowerment of the Holy Spirit. Back on campus, our disciplers trained us in sharing "the Bird Book," a simple six-page tract with a white dove on its blue cover that explains how to be filled with the Spirit.

Today, nearly two decades later, I still "breathe spiritually" and pray to be filled with the Spirit each day in obedience to Paul's command to "be filled with the Spirit" (Eph. 5:18). Some have criticized evangelicalism on the grounds of ignoring the Holy Spirit. I did not find this to be the case. My evangelical mentors constantly talked about the person and power of the Holy Spirit and our need to yield our lives to him.

Several years after I finished my seminary training, I began to develop friendships with charismatic Christians in Knoxville. These dear brothers and sisters used different words to describe their experience with the Holy Spirit. They spoke of "the Baptism" as a special encounter with the Spirit that occurs after salvation and is marked by speaking in tongues and a new empowerment for service.

Walt and Beth are a good illustration. They are winsome people with a tender passion for Christ. But they recently told me that it was formerly not that way. "Our faith had become dry, routine. We didn't share our faith with others," Beth explained. Then they received "the baptism of the Holy Spirit." They received a prayer language and a renewed love for Jesus and for the lost. "Our lives have never been the same since," Walt said. "We don't know where we would be if God hadn't touched us like that."

Literally millions of believers around the world have had similar experiences with the Holy Spirit.

HOPEFUL SIGNS

Evangelicals and Pentecostals/charismatics have argued about the Spirit's filling and baptism for nearly a century. A generation ago, much of the debate was mean-spirited: Charismatics declared that those who didn't speak in tongues were unspiritual; evangelicals accused those who claimed a Spirit-baptism as arrogant. Evangelicals have stressed the importance of being filled with the Spirit; charismatics have stressed the importance of being baptized by the Spirit. Today, however, the two sides are listening to each other—and learning.

Alister McGrath, surveying the differences between evangelicals and charismatics on this issue, is optimistic. "Each side has important contributions to make to this debate," he says. "In practice, Word and Spirit are perhaps easier to reconcile than the polarization of the debate might suggest. . . . there are excellent reasons for hoping that the next generation of evangelicalism may see an increasing maturity in both camps."[1]

The differences between the two groups are real. Charismatics believe that the baptism of the Holy Spirit comes as a second work in a believer's life. They base this on various passages in the book of Acts: 2:1–4; 8:4–25; 9:17–18; 19:1–7. They believe the Holy Spirit falls on believers *after* salvation, empowering them and giving them the gift of tongues.

Evangelicals disagree. They believe that the baptism of the Spirit comes at conversion. Evangelicals build their case on Paul's statement in 1 Corinthians 12:13: "For we were all baptized by one Spirit into one body."

Hundreds of books have been written supporting one or the other view. Yet I am convinced that the great majority of middle-of-the-road evangelicals and charismatics basically believe the same thing about the work of the Spirit. We merely use different words to describe how the Spirit works in our lives.

Can the Holy Spirit encounter us in a powerful way after salvation? Of course he can. Do we need to be filled with the Spirit on a daily basis? Of course we do. Word and power churches seek both kinds of experience.

A SPIRIT-WORK BY ANY OTHER NAME IS STILL A SPIRIT-WORK

When I first began to hear stories about "second blessings" or "deeper works," I was suspicious. Were these people running away from the hard work of spiritual discipline and hoping God would just zap them into holiness? And wasn't this just some new fad, anyway? Everyone I knew of talked about "filling." I didn't know anyone who bought into this "deeper work" teaching.

And then I did my homework. To my surprise, I found a steady stream of reports throughout church history of believers who experienced a profound, secondary Spirit-work that marked them for life. They inevitably used different terms to describe their encounter. But report after report revealed that God has been working this way for a long time. What follows is a brief sampling.

North Africa, third century. The theologian Tertullian teaches that the Holy Spirit is received after conversion through prayer and the laying on of hands.

Asia, tenth century. Symeon the New Theologian describes, in the third person, his encounter with the Holy Spirit. "One day . . . a flood of divine radiance appeared from above and filled the room, . . ." he says. "He was wounded by love and desire for [God]. . . . Oblivious of all the world he was filled with tears and with ineffable joy and gladness."[2]

Italy, fifteenth century. Savanarola, a monk with a heart to reform the church, begins preaching stirring messages on the coming judgment of God. Few respond. Then one day, while speaking with a nun,

> The great majority of middle-of-the-road evangelicals and charismatics basically believe the same thing about the work of the Spirit. We merely use different words.

he has a vision. From that moment on, his biographer tells us, "he was filled with new unction and power. His preaching was now with a voice of thunder, and his denunciation of sin so terrific that the people who listened to him sometimes went about the streets half-dazed."[3]

England, sixteenth century. The Puritans teach the doctrine of the sealing of the Spirit as a distinct work that happens after conversion. Puritan divine Thomas Goodwin writes in his commentary on Ephesians 1:13, "The work of faith is a distinct thing, a different thing from the work of assurance." Goodwin describes this second work as "the electing love of God brought home to the soul."[4]

England, eighteenth century. John Wesley, the founder of Methodism, teaches that every believer should expect two distinct experiences in their sanctification. He calls the second experience a "second blessing."

England, nineteenth century. The Higher Life movement grows rapidly, made popular by the Keswick conventions of the 1870s. Leading Bible teachers such as R. A. Torrey, D. L. Moody, Andrew Murray, and F. B. Meyer teach that the baptism of the Spirit is a secondary crisis experience empowering the believer for service. Torrey, who was Moody's disciple, writes in his book *The Baptism with the Holy Spirit*, "This is a work of the Holy Spirit separate and distinct from his regenerating work."[5]

Chicago, nineteenth century. The evangelist Dwight Moody, who founded the Moody Bible Church and Moody Bible Institute, writes two months before his death in 1899, "There are two epochs in my life that stand out clear. One is when I was between 18 and 19 years old, when I was born of the Spirit. . . . the greatest blessing, next to being born again, came 16 years after, when I was filled with the Spirit."[6]

A biography of Moody written by his son describes what happened:

> The year 1871 was a critical one in Mr. Moody's career. . . . An intense hunger and thirst for spiritual power were aroused in him by two women who used to attend meetings and sit on the front seat. . . . At the close of the services they would say to him:
> "We have been praying for you."
> "Why don't you pray for the people," Mr. Moody would ask.
> "Because you need the power of the Spirit," they would say.
> "I need the power! Why," said he, in relating the incident years after, "I thought I had the power. I had the largest congregation in Chicago, and there were many conversions. . . .

I asked them to come and talk to me and they poured out their hearts in prayer that I might receive the filling of the Holy Spirit. There came a great hunger in my soul. I did not know what it was. I began to cry out as I never did before. I really felt that I did not want to live if I could not have this power for service."

Shortly after this, Moody was in New York on a fund-raising trip.

"I was crying all the time that God would fill me with His Spirit. Well, one day, in the city of New York—oh, what a day!—I cannot describe it. I seldom refer to it; it is almost too sacred an experience to name. . . . I can only say that God revealed himself to me, and I had such an experience of his love that I had to ask him to stay his hand.

"I went to preaching again. The sermons were not different . . .yet hundreds were converted. I would not now be placed back where I was before that blessed experience if you should give me all the world."[7]

England, twentieth century. Perhaps the most surprising spokesman for a second-work teaching is the great British preacher D. Martyn Lloyd-Jones. Lloyd-Jones, who served London's Westminster Chapel for twenty-five years, has had a major influence on evangelicals. Yet Lloyd-Jones saw in the Scriptures a baptism of the Holy Spirit that was distinct from conversion. He writes, "You can be regenerate, a child of God, a true believer, and still not have received the baptism with the Holy Spirit."[8]

> Pentecostalism did not emerge in a vacuum. Significant evangelical leaders on both sides of the Atlantic were preaching a second-blessing theology.

Pentecostalism did not emerge in a vacuum. Significant evangelical leaders on both sides of the Atlantic were preaching a second-blessing theology. Pentecostalism took this teaching one step further and added tongues speaking as the initial evidence of the Baptism.

It was puzzling for me as an evangelical to see so many of my evangelical grandparents interpret the Scriptures this way. I have pored over their writings time and time again and still come down with the traditional evangelical understanding of the Baptism as occurring at conversion. Yet I also believe that these accounts, and the many more I hear personally, are true. God does touch his people in profound ways long after they are saved. Regardless of the terms we use to describe these experiences, we all know that God is sovereign—that he is able to give his children special touches resulting in giant spiritual leaps forward. He may even do it more than once in a person's life. And he doesn't have to do it the same way each time.

JERRY'S STORY

Several years ago a friend in my accountability group came to a place in his life where he was desperate for God's touch. Jerry was broken. His marriage was in trouble. Guilt over a past, often-confessed sin was tormenting him. He was failing as a father. He confessed his plight to the men in his accountability group, received prayer and some hugs, and then caught a plane for a business trip. A friend he knew in the city where he was staying called him and invited him to go to church with him on Sunday morning. Toward the end of the service, the pastor shared a prophetic word Jerry knew applied to him. He went forward and told the pastor, "I'm the man you were talking about."

"Can I pray for you?" the pastor asked.

"Please."

The pastor laid hands on Jerry and prayed for him in his spiritual language. "I went out cold," Jerry told me. "Time stopped." He lay on the floor, overwhelmed by the love of God. Nearly a half hour went by. When he awoke, he was a changed man. I know Jerry well and can say that his spiritual growth developed more in those thirty minutes than it did in all the years I have known him.

Several years have passed now, and the fruit of Jerry's encounter with Christ is lasting and real. Jerry used to have a hard time fitting in daily quiet times. Now he spends hours in the Scriptures. Before his encounter, Jerry couldn't figure out where he fit in ministry and spent many hours in hobbies and projects that were enjoyable to him but had little kingdom impact. Today Jerry and his wife are among Fellowship's strongest leaders. "When I'm in town, I want to invest my time in the people I'm shepherding," Jerry says. And he does.

We call these dramatic encounters "deeper works of the Spirit" or "special fillings of the Spirit." If you want to call them the baptism of the Holy Spirit, I won't argue with you. Call them what you want. But I believe in them.

MIKE'S STORY

For each great Christian who had a "second blessing" that rocketed him or her into superior service, you can probably find a great Christian who did not. Many times it is God's plan to sanctify us in less dramatic ways than some of the stories above relate.

I have asked each member of my staff to send out a monthly prayer letter to his or her personal intercessory team. They send me copies. Mike's recent prayer letter was eloquent and moving, revealing a heart firmly in the grip of God's hand. I set Mike's letter down on my desk and said aloud, "Wow, has he ever grown!"

Mike left a high-paying management position to join the church staff eight years ago. He is not the same man who signed on in 1991. He loves people with greater compassion. He worships with more intensity. He cares more about his next-door neighbor who doesn't know the Lord. He leads with greater wisdom. He hears God's voice with more clarity and assurance.

Mike's growth has been a steady, quiet progression fueled by prayer, fasting, time in the Scriptures, and the encouragement of a few choice friends, especially his wife. The story of Mike's journey is filled with little choices—specifically, each day choosing to be filled with the Holy Spirit. There have been no dramatic spiritual encounters in Mike's journey, no "deeper works" such as the one Jerry experienced. Yet he and Jerry are both making good progress on the road to holiness.

The Spirit is sovereign.

SOFTER LINES

The lines that have traditionally divided us are softening. This is especially true when it comes to our terminology for describing the work of the Spirit. One leader of a national organization that works with both charismatics and evangelicals told me this week, "Ten years from now we won't even use the terms anymore. The distinctions are blurring. This is what God is doing around the world."

Imagine for a moment that this leader is correct: The two great traditions seek out a middle way that embraces the best of both while celebrating their own distinctive tradition. What will these churches teach about the ministry of the Spirit?

BE FILLED WITH THE SPIRIT

Late one February night I pulled down from the Lee College library shelf an original copy of the biography of D. L. Moody, written by his son. The book's faded green cover crackled when I bent it open, revealing brittle, yellowed pages. I skimmed through the earlier sections of his life until my eyes caught the paragraph about Moody's dramatic encounter with the Spirit. It was a sacred moment. Somehow the yellowness of the book's pages spoke a special nearness to Moody and his times. Like Lucy, Edmund, Susan, and Peter in *The Chronicles of Narnia,* I walked through the wardrobe into another world.

It was 1871. These were days of power and hope in the kingdom of God. Charles G. Finney had just finished an astonishing career of revivalism. The church, revived with the optimistic hope that it would bring in the kingdom of God, had been challenging every social issue from slavery to women's rights. Men like Andrew Murray were writing classics that would warm hearts for more than a century. Amy Carmichael was beginning her life's work in India, Hudson Taylor was about to open China to the gospel, and a young cricketer named C. T. Studd was calling thousands of students onto the foreign mission field. Charles Spurgeon was thundering eloquently from the Metropolitan Tabernacle pulpit. And Moody was winning souls.

> The church seemed to be triumphant, more than conquerors, a force to be reckoned with. What was the secret?

The church seemed to be triumphant, more than conquerors, a force to be reckoned with, optimistic, confident, speaking with authority to the day's great issues rather than existing in exile on the fringes of popular culture. What was the secret?

I read Moody's story closely, scanning each line again and again. Several lines refused to recede back into their pages and beckoned me to ponder them.

"Mr. Moody, you need the power of the Spirit." Do I, Lord? Am I where Mr. Moody was?

"...had such an experience of love I had to ask God to stay his hand." Lord, could that happen to me, too?

"...hundreds were saved." Oh, God, how I long for that kind of fruit in my ministry!

I returned the book to the shelf and headed out into the winter night.

The next day a retired missionary working as a librarian asked me if I wanted to go to a Pentecostal revival service that night. "The Lord's been working mightily," she said, stuffing a flyer in my hand. "You ought to go." So I did.

Will tonight be the night? I wondered. *Will I experience the powerful filling Moody described?* I arrived early and took a seat on the right of the sanctuary, far enough back to escape if necessary, but close enough to see what was going on. I had never heard a real-life Pentecostal revival speaker before, and my imagination had gotten the best of me. Would he be like Jimmy Swaggert? Kathryn Kuhlman? Benny Hinn?

When the speaker came to the pulpit, after a half hour of worship similar to what we enjoy at Fellowship, I was disappointed. He looked, well, like a normal guy. About my age. Receding hair line. Pretty wife playing the piano.

He was introduced as an evangelist, but his message was not for the lost. Nor was it a sermon for the saved, at least in the way I had always defined them. It was more a rhythmic, driving, spiritual rap, like the kind of preaching one hears in the movie *The Apostle*. When the speaker finished, fifty-five minutes later, he called the congregation forward for prayer. I sensed sincerity in his passion and tears. I sensed purity in the faces of those around me. This was a safe place to meet God.

I joined about fifty others who were seeking prayer. He wandered among us, praying for healing for some, for "the Baptism" for others. Then his eyes met mine. He pressed through several teenagers and stood before me.

Here it comes, I thought. *Lord, stir my passion. Give me an anointing to serve you. I don't really believe in the Baptism the way he does, but give me one anyway!*

His voice raspy from nearly an hour of rapid-fire preaching, he asked me if he could pray for me.

"Yes," I said.

He placed his hands on my head and prayed, first in English, then in his spiritual language. I sensed the Spirit's gentle presence. I sensed God was pleased. I sensed I was there to learn something.

I didn't sense much else.

No deeper works were in store for me that night. I didn't experience such an overwhelming love that I had to ask God to stay his hand.

I headed out into the night alone, cold, and disappointed. I thought, *If I can't get a touch of the Spirit at a Pentecostal revival meeting, I'm hopeless.*

Several years have passed, and although I have asked God for special works in my life, this has not been his plan. But I have learned something from my experience. I have learned of the danger of taking someone else's spiritual story and trying to make it my own. And I have learned to focus on those areas I am responsible for.

I can't make God bless me with a profound spiritual experience: That's *his* choice. I can choose to be filled with the Spirit: That's *my* choice. Reading stories about other people's spiritual encounters can be encouraging, but it also can be dangerous. I found there was a fine line in my longing for a Moody-style experience between sincerely wanting to be more effective for God and wanting to take a spiritual shortcut to holiness.

> Word and power churches must tell their people that there are no shortcuts.

Whether we like it or not, the Christian life is, as Eugene Peterson put it, "a long obedience in the same direction." Spiritual growth is normally a long, slow, journey. Only rarely is it a dramatic boost forward. "Train yourself to be godly," Paul told Timothy (1 Tim. 4:7). The word Paul uses is the root for our word *gymnasium*. It means "to discipline yourself, to work out, to exercise." It means sweating.

Word and power churches must tell their people that there are no shortcuts.

Psychiatrist M. Scott Peck observes,

> There are many people I know who possess a vision of [personal] evolution yet seem to lack the will for it. They want, and believe it is possible, to skip over the discipline, to find an easy shortcut to sainthood. Some attempt to attain it by simply imitating the superficialities of saints, retiring to the desert or taking up carpentry. Some even believe that by such imitation they have really become saints and prophets, and are unable to acknowledge that they are still children and face the painful fact that they must start at the beginning and go through the middle.[9]

Spiritual growth is hard work. We are to "press on toward the goal" and "run the race with endurance," to "put to death the deeds of the body" and "pick up our cross." Spiritual progress is made when we make those hard daily choices to be filled with the Spirit and to say no to the flesh.

The spiritual disciplines are the way by which we are filled with the Holy Spirit. "A discipline for the spiritual life is nothing but an activity undertaken to bring us into more effective cooperation with Christ and his kingdom," explains Dallas Willard. "Spiritual disciplines make us capable of receiving more of his life and power."[10]

PRAYING FOR THE RELEASE OF SPIRITUAL GIFTS

When an understanding of the progressive nature of sanctification is firmly in place, it is safe to ask the question, What about deeper works? Do we just hope they happen, or do we actively pray for them?

Paul evidently believed that prayer with the laying on of hands did, at least on occasion, impart or stir up spiritual gifts. "Do not neglect your gift," Paul challenged Timothy, "which was *given you* through a prophetic message when the body of elders laid their hands on you" (1 Tim 4:14). Several years later Paul followed up that plea with a similar one: "Fan into flame the gift of God, *which is in you* through the laying on of my hands" (2 Tim. 1:6). Timothy was clearly already a believer when he received the prayer from Paul that imparted to him a spiritual gift. New Testament scholar F. F. Bruce explains, "The imposition of hands was an early Christian practice associated especially with the impartation of the Holy Spirit."[11]

Spiritual gifts are given to empower us to minister. The setting of Timothy's prayer appears to be his commissioning to work with the church in Ephesus. Evidently, the elders and Paul prayed that certain spiritual gifts would be released in Timothy to enable him to fulfill his calling. This was not merely a prayer for the filling of the Spirit. This was a prayer for a special empowerment, for new giftings that were not present in Timothy before.

We can follow the early church's example by praying for those whom we are sending into ministry. We should lay hands on them and ask the Holy Spirit to impart to them the spiritual gifts they need to fulfill their calling.

The typical "commissioning" service is often ritualistic instead of empowering. Timothy's commissioning was so powerful that, years later, Paul urged him to draw strength by remembering the gifts he received that day. Missionaries are sent overseas with sincere prayers for safety and fruitfulness. Think how much more effective they would be if we pleaded with God to release in them powerful cross-cultural evangelistic giftings?

The church growth movement introduced inventory testings to help believers identify their spiritual gifts. The Network movement took us even further by providing resources and training to help believers not only identify their spiritual gifts, but match them with a place of ministry in the church.

Could there be another step in releasing people into effective ministry—laying hands on them and praying for any special giftings they need to do the job? I am not an evangelist and do not feel I have led Fellowship well in this regard. So while preaching a series on evangelism, I asked for a group to pray for a release of evangelistic gifts in me.

I still am no Billy Graham, but within months God gave me several friendships with men who are spiritually seeking. We are becoming good friends. One of my friends came to Christ last December, and I had the opportunity to baptize him on New Year's Eve. God has given me a real love for these men and they for me.

PRAYING FOR FULLNESS

When I hear or read of someone's "baptism of the Spirit," I immediately think of Paul's prayer for the Ephesians.

> I pray that out of his glorious riches he may strengthen you with power through his Spirit in your inner being, so that Christ may dwell in your hearts through faith. And I pray that you, being rooted and established in love, may have power, together with all the saints, to grasp how wide and long and high and deep is the love of Christ, and to know this love that surpasses knowledge—that you may be filled to the measure of all the fullness of God. (Eph. 3:16–19)

Look at what Paul prays for.

Power
Love
Filling
Fullness

The deeper works I know of are simply dramatic answers to Paul's prayer for the Ephesians. Should we pray for this? Of course! These are biblical prayers. What we cannot control is the way that God answers these prayers. Some may experience God's power, love, filling, and fullness in a dramatic, crisis-type event. Most will experience these blessings in a gradual but ever-increasing measure.

After the service one Sunday morning, several of us prayed for a young woman who was preparing to spend her summer in a rigorous leadership training program. "All I want right now is to love God. Would you pray that nothing would choke out my passion for him?" We began to pray Ephesians 3 over her. Quietly she began to experience God's love for her in a way she had never known before. "This is incredible!" she said. "He's holding me. It's so sweet. I want to stay here forever."

What label should we give this young woman's encounter with the Spirit?

Let's just call it "answered prayer."

STUDY QUESTIONS

1. "The great majority of middle-of-the-road evangelicals and charismatics basically believe the same thing about the work of the Spirit." Do you agree? Discuss your answer.

2. What are the implications of knowing that so many evangelicals had dynamic charismatic experiences? What does this mean for evangelicals? for charismatics?

3. Do you agree that second blessings are wonderful, empowering experiences *and* that the persistent work of the spiritual work can never be replaced? How does this affect your walk with God?

4. Does your church depend on the empowerment of the Spirit? How can you encourage sincere prayer for the Spirit's presence among you?

EPILOGUE

This book is for Sandi, my beloved wife. Sandi, I don't remember much about the summer of '81, but I do remember falling in love with you. I had never met a girl quite like you. Nothing was more important to you than loving and serving God. I had never met anyone as disciplined as you were. You rose at 5:30 each morning for hour-long quiet times, memorized Scripture, discipled a number of your fellow students, shared your faith each week, made great grades, and worked twenty hours a week on the side. The only time I could be alone with you was to pretend I wanted to go witnessing—and then get you talking.

You kept up these heroic spiritual efforts for the first years of our marriage, through four children, through the rigors of planting a church, through our daughter's battle with cancer. And then your soul began to ache for more. We began to talk about the Father's love and your saying how little you experienced it. We began to talk about what it would be like not just to know *about* God, but to really know him—personally, intimately, passionately. Many nights, you wept in frustration as you peered into the canyon that lay between what you knew in your head and what you felt in your heart.

Then the Spirit began to awaken a part of your heart that had been asleep for many years. He gave you the freedom to dance again. You are never more beautiful to me than when you are worshiping God in dance. I have never seen you more passionate! He gave you a circle of friends with whom you have carefully and tenderly pursued the things of the Spirit. He gave you a prayer language. You are experiencing the prophetic. You are learning how to listen to God in prayer and move into others' lives in powerful ways. I loved who you were when I married you. I love even more who you are and who you are becoming. This book is for you.

↝

This book is for David, my neighbor. David, I have never told you this, but you are partly responsible for messing up my theology.

You were one of the people God brought into my life when my understanding of the spiritual gifts was being turned upside down. You surprised me with your story of your own dramatic encounter with the Holy Spirit and your testimony of how the charismatic renewal brought you to faith.

I have been watching you for several years now, first as my neighbor and then as a new member of Fellowship church. You and your wife were devoted, faithful members of a wonderful charismatic church here in town. You gave your life and soul to that church. I watched you struggle as your time drew to a close there. You loved that church and still do. Yet something was missing. It was an ache for truth, you said, a cry for balance, a yearning to anchor your experience of God to the authority of his Word. Quietly and with tears, you left your precious church and came to ours.

I watched you leave the house the other morning well before dawn. You were heading off to spend two hours poring over the Scriptures with a handful of guys you've chosen to give two years of your life to. That group has changed you, David. You can't stop talking about what you are learning in the Word. There is fire in the fireplace again. Your spiritual journey has resumed.

This book is for you, David. And even more importantly, it is for the great people and great pastors in the church you left.

⌒

This book is for Art, my friend. Art, I have become quite fond of you since we met last year. I think we were both a little wary of one another at first. Do you remember asking me if I was going to try to convert you? Your intense spiritual hunger encourages me in my own pursuit of God. When I asked you what your life passion is, you didn't even have to think about your answer. "To know God," you said. And I believe you.

You have not found God, though, in the Christian church. "Why did you leave?" I probed one Friday afternoon after you related that you had grown up in a traditional evangelical church. "Because I was looking for a God who would talk to me," you said. "And I didn't find him there." You then told me your story—the years in divinity school, the pain of spiritual rejection by conservative Christians, the time in Paris with the Buddhist priest that marked your life forever. And the longing—the insatiable longing for a God you could experience. Your life, as far as I can tell, is an all-out quest to encounter a talking God. I admire you for that, Art.

You asked me once about my own spirituality. No, you were more specific than that. You wanted to know if I spoke in tongues. When I told you I did, we talked about it for half an hour. Something about my story seemed to intersect with your story.

This book is for you, Art. It describes a church that is different from the one that failed you as a boy. It describes a church that is different from the ones that hurt you even today. It describes a community where God is encountered as well as discussed, felt as well as believed. It invites you into a community where people really do believe God talks.

ARE MIRACULOUS GIFTS FOR TODAY?

This appendix is painful to write. My heart in this book has been to unite, not divide. I have tried to point out areas of agreement rather than stressful areas where believers differ. Yet theology does matter, and this whole book is built on the theological assumption that the miraculous gifts mentioned in 1 Corinthians 12:7–11 are for today. Some readers will need to go deeper in examining this assumption. Here is the passage in question:

> Now to each one the manifestation of the Spirit is given for the common good. To one there is given through the Spirit the message of wisdom, to another the message of knowledge by means of the same Spirit, to another faith by the same Spirit, to another gifts of healing by that one Spirit, to another miraculous powers, to another prophecy, to another distinguishing between spirits, to another speaking in different kinds of tongues, and to still another the interpretation of tongues. All these are the work of one and the same Spirit, and he gives them to each one, just as he determines.

Some in the body of Christ hold a cessationist position about these gifts.

The cessationist position argues that there are no miraculous gifts of the Holy Spirit today. Gifts such as prophecy, tongues, and healing were confined to the first century and were used at the time the apostles were establishing churches and the New Testament was not complete.[1]

I was taught this view in seminary by some of the godliest, most humble, and most scholarly men I know. I bristle when those who accept the miraculous gifts portray those who don't as mean-spirited, Spirit-quenching Pharisees. My professors were not Pharisees! They knew God intimately and walked in the power of the Holy Spirit. I find no pleasure in disagreeing with men I respect and love so much. My prayer is that the following pages will be written with gentleness and respect for a tradition that has meant much to me.

Nearly every evangelical pastor I know who was taught the doctrine of cessation in seminary has since rejected it.

These pastors and I have traveled a path similar to one Dr. John Piper described to his congregation in a series of sermons he was preaching on the miraculous gifts. Dr. Piper is the pastor of Bethlehem Baptist Church in Minneapolis and a seminary professor at Bethel Seminary. On February 25, 1990, Dr. Piper preached a sermon titled "Are Signs and Wonders for Today?" He began by holding up two stacks of books. One stack represented the cessation tradition, the other stack the view that God still gives the miraculous gifts today. After reviewing the arguments from both points of view, he concluded by holding up the cessationist books.

> I find in this tradition virtually every teacher that I've loved and benefited from. . . . I love these men. They are my kind of people. But I don't find their arguments compelling. . . . Even when I was a 15-year-old boy lying in bed in Greenville, South Carolina, listening to M. R. DeHaan preach [on cessation] from 1 Corinthians 13, I thought to myself, "That won't work." It never has worked for me.[2]

Most biblical scholars have come to the same conclusion. Gordon Fee, professor of New Testament at Regent Seminary in Vancouver, told me, "This is a dead issue in the academy. Hardly anyone is defending [cessation] anymore." A leader from a strong, conservative evangelical denomination recently told me that only one of its top twenty national leaders still held to the doctrine of cessation. The *Eternity* editorial cited earlier is worth remembering. "More and more evangelical scholars today," wrote the editors of this evangelical publication in 1973, "feel that the traditional, supposed biblical arguments for the cessation of the gifts after completion of the New Testament cannot be sustained by the Holy Scripture."[3]

THE CASE FOR CESSATIONISM

This appendix summarizes and responds to the main arguments for the doctrine of cessation. It is more technical than the body of the book and cites many sources for those who desire more study.

1. 1 Corinthians 13:8–13 teaches that the miraculous gifts passed away with the completion of the New Testament. Paul wrote 1 Corinthians 12–14 to answer questions the Corinthians were having about the use and abuse of spiritual gifts in their fellowship. His primary goal was to encourage the Corinthians to love one another. Chapter 13 describes the supremacy of love over any other gift. Paul's purpose in 1 Corinthians 13:8–13 is to show that love is greater than any gift:

> Love never fails. But where there are prophecies, they will cease; where there are tongues, they will be stilled; where there is knowledge, it will pass away. For we know in part and we prophesy in part, but when perfection comes, the imperfect disappears. When I was a child I talked like a child, I thought like a child, I reasoned like a child. When I became a man I put childish ways behind me. Now we see but a poor reflection as in a mirror; then we shall see face to face. Now I know in part; then I shall know fully, even as I am fully known. And now these three remain: faith, hope and love. But the greatest of these is love.

The miraculous gifts such as tongues and prophecy will cease. But when? "When perfection comes." When perfection comes, these imperfect gifts will pass away. To what is Paul referring when he looks to the coming of "perfection"? There are basically two ways scholars have interpreted this passage.

Cessationists argue that "perfection" refers to the completed canon of Scripture. They hold that the first-century church needed these miraculous revelatory gifts because the Bible was not yet complete, and when God completed the scriptural canon, these gifts were no longer needed and passed away.[4]

Noncessationists believe that "perfection" refers to the second coming of Christ. They hold that these gifts are intended for the present church age but will no longer be needed when Jesus Christ returns. The majority of biblical interpreters have concluded that "perfection" refers to the second coming of Christ and not the completion of the canon.[5] How have they reached this conclusion?

a. Paul says that when the perfect comes, we will see God "face to face." The phrase "face to face" is used in the Old Testament to mean seeing God personally.[6] Revelation 22:4 says that in heaven, "They will see his face." The Scriptures reveal much about God, but they do not allow for a *face-to-face* meeting with him. This will come when Christ returns.

b. Paul says that, for us, when perfection comes, "I shall know fully, even as I am fully known." The Scriptures help us know many things, but it could not be said that we know God *fully* because of them. God will be known fully to his people when his Son returns.

Lloyd-Jones rejects the view that the word *perfect* refers to the closed canon:

> [Do] you see what that involves? It means that you and I who have the Scriptures open before us, know much more than the apostle Paul of God's truth . . . if that argument is correct. It means that we are altogether superior to the early church and even to the apostles themselves, including the apostle Paul! . . . The "then" is the glory everlasting. It is only then that I shall know, even as also I am known; for then I shall see Him as He is.[7]

c. It is doubtful that when the Corinthians read this letter, the concept of a closed canon would have occurred to them. A far more common theme in Scripture is the return of Christ. When Paul pointed his Corinthian readers to a future day when they would see Christ face to face, they are far more likely to have thought of Christ's return.

For these reasons, and many others[8] treated in the scholarly literature[9], the most reasonable interpretation of 1 Corinthians 13:8–12 says that Paul is teaching that the gifts will cease when Jesus Christ returns.[10] Lloyd-Jones concludes his summary of the cessation arguments with typical bluntness:

> Let me begin to answer by giving you just one thought. . . . The Scriptures never anywhere say that these things were only temporary—never! There is no such statement anywhere. . . . So you see the difficulties men land themselves in when they dislike something and cannot fully understand it and try to explain it away. All things must be judged in the light of the Scriptures, and we must not twist them to suit our theory or argument.[11]

2. The miraculous gifts ceased with the death of the last apostle. B. B. Warfield, a professor at Princeton Seminary, wrote a book in 1918 called *Counterfeit Miracles,* which is still the classic statement of the position that the miraculous spiritual gifts were given only to the apostles and Stephen and Philip. Warfield taught that the purpose of these gifts was to authenticate the apostles as trustworthy bearers of doctrine; when they died, this authenticating power died with them. Most of the contemporary works written from the cessationist camp are, in effect, a footnote to Warfield's work. Warfield wrote,

> It is very clear from the record of the New Testament that the extraordinary charismata were not (after the very first days of the church) the possession of all Christians, but supernatural gifts to the few.[12]
>
> These gifts were not the possession of the primitive Christian as such: nor for that matter of the Apostolic Church or the Apostolic age for themselves; they were distinctly for the authentication of the Apostles. They were part of the credentials of the Apostles as the authoritative agents of God in founding the church. Their function thus confined them to distinctively the Apostolic Church, and they necessarily passed away with it.[13]

The primary texts used by cessationists to support the claim that miraculous gifts were the sole property of the apostles include these:

> "The apostles performed many miraculous signs and wonders among the people" (Acts 5:12).
> "The signs that mark an apostle—signs, wonders and miracles—were done among you" (2 Cor. 12:12).
> "This salvation, which was first announced by the Lord, was confirmed to us by those who heard him. God also testified to it by signs, wonders and various miracles and gifts of the Holy Spirit" (Heb. 2:3–4).

Warfield is correct in affirming the uniqueness of the apostolic office. The twelve apostles served a unique foundational role in redemptive history. Scripture does seem at pains to show that the apostles enjoyed a unique wonder-working power.

The major problem with Warfield's argument, however, is that its conclusion does not follow from its premises. The argument can be broken down into a syllogism.

Major premise: The apostles, as the foundation of the church, experienced unique wonder-working powers to authenticate their ministry.

Minor premise: The apostles are dead.

Conclusion: No one experiences wonder-working power in ministry today.[14]

The conclusion does not follow from the minor premise. While it is true that the apostles had unique miraculous powers and it is true that they are dead, it does not logically follow that no other Christians can experience the miraculous gifts. Jack Deere points out how flawed this reasoning is when he applies it to church planting. We could say:

Major premise: Only the apostles planted churches in Acts.

Minor premise: The apostles are dead.

Conclusion: No one should plant churches today.[15]

All that is needed to refute this view from a scriptural standpoint is to find any examples of nonapostolic Christians using the miraculous gifts in the New Testament. Consider these:

Mark 9:38–39: An unknown man casts out demons in Jesus' name.

Luke 10:9: Jesus commissions seventy-two disciples to preach and to heal.

Acts 9:17–18: Ananias heals Paul.

Romans 12:6: Paul refers to the gift of prophecy in Rome, a church not yet visited by an apostle.

1 Corinthians 12:8–10: Gifts of healing and miracles are experienced in the Corinthian church without an apostle present.

Galatians 3:5: Paul refers to the Holy Spirit who "work[s] miracles among you." The "you" is plural and must refer to the entire congregation, which was not led by an apostle.

1 Thessalonians 5:20: Paul demands that the Thessalonians not hinder the prophetic gift.

The list of miraculous gifts experienced by nonapostles in the New Testament grows much longer when we include tongues.

Even a progressive dispensationalist like Dr. Robert Saucy of Talbot School of Theology, who stresses in his writings the uniqueness of the apostolic era, challenges cessationist logic at this point:

While agreeing with many of the emphases in the cessationist position, some of the conclusions that demand the complete cessation of miraculous gifts in my opinion go beyond the express teaching of Scripture or necessary deductions from theological principles of Scripture.[16]

While the unique ministry of the apostles is honored and revered, it cannot be inferred from that ministry that the miraculous gifts were limited to and died with them.[17]

3. Allowing miraculous gifts such as prophecy undermines the sufficiency of Scripture. This argument is concerned with protecting the Scriptures as the final and authoritative revelation of God's inerrant Word. John MacArthur makes this argument at the beginning of his case against the charismatics, with the question, "Is the Bible still being written?"[18]

> Christians on both sides of the Charismatic fence must realize a vital truth: God's revelation is finished for now. . . . God's Word is complete. Jude encompasses the entire New Testament when he writes: "Once for all delivered to the saints" (Jude 3). . . . God worked through a certain historical process to establish the authenticity of the canon so we might have a clear standard. If we now throw out that historical process and redefine inspiration and revelation, we undermine the standard which God gave us. If we then undermine the uniqueness of the Bible, we will have no way of distinguishing God's voice from man's voice. Eventually anyone can say anything and claim it is God's Word, and no one will have the right to refute it.[19]

MacArthur's concern is well-founded. The history of the church records numerous spurious groups that plunged into heresy when they became unanchored from Scripture and began "hearing God." He also levels fair criticism at a charismatic movement that, in practice, too often seems to equate "a word from God" with scriptural authority. Furthermore, noncessationists agree that the Scriptures are fully sufficient and that there is no new authoritative revelation being given today.

This argument would be true if the New Testament gift of prophecy were like Old Testament prophecy in its authority. If Paul intended to teach in 1 Corinthians 12:8–10 that some in the body would have gifts to speak for God just as authoritatively as Isaiah or Jeremiah did, then we would agree that those gifts have passed away. God is not writing new Scripture today.

But as we have seen, New Testament prophecy is not equal to Scripture in authority, and no responsible noncessationist claims that contemporary prophetic gifts have such authority. George Mallone writes, "To my knowledge no noncessationist in the mainstream of Christianity claims that revelation today is equal with Scripture."[20]

MacArthur has too narrowly defined the word *revelation* (*apoka-lypsis*) as always referring to scriptural revelation, when in fact it does not. Describing a Corinthian church service, Paul writes in 1 Corinthians 14:26, "When you come together, everyone has a hymn, or a word of instruction, a revelation, a tongue or an interpretation." Clearly, Paul did not mean that people were speaking with Old Testament prophetic authority! If so, why did Paul demand that these revelations be tested by the assembly?

In the New Testament, the word *reveal* is not always used in reference to Scripture. It can simply mean "divinely prompted guidance or direction." Paul says that "God will make clear" to the Philippians the nature of their attitude (Phil. 3:15). Paul prays for the Ephesians "that the God of our Lord Jesus Christ, the glorious Father, may give you the Spirit of wisdom and revelation, so that you may know him better" (Eph. 1:17).

The word *apokalypsis* is not confined in Paul's writing to the foundation message of Christ. In Galatians 2:2 Paul reports that he traveled to Jerusalem to the Apostolic Council on the basis of a revelation:

> He undertook the journey on the basis of divine direction. . . . such a revelation can be shared by other Spirit-filled Christians. . . . This is the explanation of Paul's prayer that God might give the Ephesians "the Spirit of wisdom and revelation."[21]

Pressing MacArthur's arguments to their logical conclusion, one would have to do away with the illuminating, guiding ministry of the Holy Spirit altogether, for these would compromise the sufficiency of Scripture. Yet it is widely agreed that the possibility of being guided by God in prayer does not compromise Scripture, for it is an entirely different type of revelation altogether.

4. Church history proves that all evidence of the miraculous gifts passed away after the first century. This argument filled the bulk of Warfield's pages and has been popular in cessationist writing ever since. Two responses are in order. First, even if it could be proved that the gifts passed away in the history of the church, this does not prove that God will not grant them again. Second, history does not prove that the miraculous gifts passed away, as we will see below.[22]

Stanley Burgess has produced a three-volume study on the history of the doctrine of the Holy Spirit. He writes, "Before John Chrysostom (A.D. 347–407) in the East and Augustine of Hippo (A.D. 354–430) in the West, no church father suggested that any or all of the charismata were intended only for the first-century Church."[23]

The Patristic Era (A.D. 100–600). An early second-century document, *The Didache,* was written to ministers. It exhorted the church to "permit the prophets to give thanks as much as they desire" and then proceeded to give instruction on how prophetic utterances were to be tested.[24] Justin Martyr (ca. A.D. 100–165) reminds fellow Christians in a letter that "many of our Christian men . . . have healed and do heal, rendering helpless and driving the possessing devils out."[25] Irenaeus (ca. A.D. 130–202) writes,

> We do also hear many brethren in the Church who possess prophetic gifts, and who through the Spirit speak all kinds of languages, and bring to light for the general benefit the hidden things of men. . . . those who are in truth His disciples . . . do certainly and truly drive out devils, so that those who have thus been cleansed from evil spirits frequently both believe and join themselves to the Church. Others have foreknowledge of things to come; they see visions. . . . others still heal the sick by laying their hands upon them, and they are made whole. Yea, moreover, as I have said, the dead even have been raised up and remained among us for many years.[26]

Origen, writing in the third century, reported that signs and wonders validated the proclamation of the gospel:

> The Gospel has a demonstration of its own. . . . this . . . method is called by the apostle the "manifestation of the Spirit and of power:" of "the Spirit" on account of the prophecies, which are sufficient to produce faith in any one who reads them . . . and of "power", because of the signs and wonders.[27]

The Latin theologian Hilary of Poitiers, writing in the fourth century, affirmed that the miraculous gifts were operating in his day:

> The gift of the Spirit is manifest . . . where there is . . . the gift of healings, that by the cure of disease we should bear witness to His grace . . . or by the working of miracles . . . or

by prophecy . . . or by discerning of spirits . . . or by kinds of tongues, that the speaking in tongues may be bestowed as a sign of the gift of the Holy Spirit; or by the interpretation of tongues.[28]

Finally, Augustine, who wrote in the late fourth and early fifth century, believed that the gift of tongues was not given to the church in his day, but that the gift of miracles was. In a fascinating chapter in *The City of God*, Augustine writes of numerous healings, exorcisms, and visions and says, regarding his own congregation,

> . . . many miracles were wrought, the same God who wrought those we read of still performing them. . . . One miracle was wrought among ourselves. . . . I suppose there is no inhabitant of Hippo who did not either see or hear of it. . . . There were seven brothers and three sisters . . . all of them seized with a hideous shaking of their limbs. . . . Two of them came to Hippo. . . . They came daily to the church, and specially to the relics of the most glorious Stephen praying that God might now be appeased, and restore their former health. . . . Easter arrived, and on the Lord's day . . . the young man was holding the bars of the holy place where the relics were, and praying suddenly he fell down, and lay precisely as if asleep, but not trembling as he was wont to do even in sleep. All present were astonished. . . . And behold! He rose up, and trembled no more, for he was healed.[29]

The Medieval Era (600–1500). Colette of Corbi (d. 1447) founded a convent and earned a reputation as one through whom God worked in miraculous ways. *The Lives of the Saints* tells us that the Duchess of Bourbon believed that she resuscitated the dead and comments that ". . . the fame of the miracles and labours of the carpenter's daughter was in every mouth."[30]

The lives of the saints are filled with stories of the miraculous. Modern-day Protestant scholarship tends to discredit these accounts as legends, but this reactionary approach to church history betrays modernist presuppositions about what sorts of things could and could not have happened in a saint's life.

One other example of the presence of gifts during this period is the Scholastic mystical theologian Joachim of Fiore (d. 1202), who wrote in his theology of the Holy Spirit that the Spirit spoke through prophets and that the gift of tongues is imparted by the Holy Spirit by means of the imposition of hands.[31]

The Reformation and the Modern Era (1500 to present). It is widely reported that the Reformers did not believe in the miraculous gifts. The Roman Catholic Church buttressed their authority on claims of miracles, many of which the Reformers questioned. Therefore it is somewhat surprising to find Martin Luther writing the following advice to a pastor who sought his counsel in ministering to a sick man:

> I know of no worldly advice to give. If the physicians are at a loss to find a remedy, you may be sure that it is not a case of ordinary melancholy. It must, rather, be an affliction that comes from the devil and must be counteracted by the power of Christ and the prayer of faith.
>
> Accordingly you should proceed as follows.... Graciously deign to free this man from all evil, and bring to naught the work that Satan has done in him.... Then, when you depart, lay your hands on the man again and say, "These signs shall follow them that believe; they shall lay hands on the sick, and they shall recover."[32]

In this century, D. Martyn Lloyd-Jones helped to foster a renewed interest in Reformation theology in general and the Puritan way of thought in particular. He writes:

> There is evidence from many of those Protestant Reformers and Fathers, that some of them had a genuine, true gift of prophecy.... read these books.... you will find this gift of prophecy ... [and] the occasional miracle. Anyone who is prepared to say that all this ended with the apostolic age, and that there has never been a miracle since the apostles ... gives the lie ... [and] is to quench the Holy Spirit.[33]

It is probably fair to say that the power churches have seen too much of the miraculous in the history of the church, and the word church has seen too little. (There is no entry under "miracle" in the subject index of Philip Schaff's *History of the Christian Church.*) As is so often the case, the truth appears to be somewhere in the middle. God has continued to give the miraculous gifts throughout the history of the church, although in varying degrees. There is a growing scholarly literature developing supporting this conclusion.[34]

5. The miraculous gifts were given only during the three periods of history when new revelation was given. Therefore, they are not being given today. John MacArthur teaches this view:

> Most biblical miracles happened in three relatively brief periods of Bible history: in the days of Moses and Joshua, during the miracles of Elijah and Elisha, and in the time of Christ and the apostles.... All three periods of miracles were given in times when God gave his written revelation—Scripture, in substantial quantities.[35]

The major problem with this argument is that a great number of supernatural events occur outside of these three periods.[36] What is more, even if it is shown that the miraculous decreased at certain times, there may be other reasons for the decline, such as rebellion and sin. Samuel Storms makes a telling criticism of this argument:

> At most this might suggest that in three periods of redemptive history, miraculous phenomena were more prevalent than at other times. This fact does not prove that miraculous phenomena in other times were nonexistent, nor does it prove that an increase in miraculous phenomena could not appear in subsequent phases of redemptive history.[37]

Note how far removed from specific Scripture texts the debate has become at this point. The doctrine of cessationism hangs on the slender threads of deductive reasoning. There are simply no supporting texts.

6. Jesus says, "A wicked and adulterous generation looks for a miraculous sign" (Matt. 16:4). This means that we should not pray for the miraculous in our ministries today. The problem with this objection is that it fails to consider who Jesus' audience was. Matthew 16 shows us that the "wicked and adulterous generation" referred to were the Scribes and the Pharisees who came to test Jesus by asking for a sign. Jesus was rebuking hard-hearted unbelievers who mocked him with this request. Notice the greater frequency with which Jesus compassionately responded to a request for a miracle.

Significantly, Acts 4:30 relates that the apostles and the early disciples prayed for signs and wonders to follow their preaching ministry. Paul, rather than discouraging his readers from seeking the miraculous gifts, told them to desire them eagerly (1 Cor. 14:1). John writes that "many people saw the miraculous signs he was doing and believed in his name" (John 2:23). Then he reinforces the positive role of signs in proclaiming the gospel: "Jesus did many other miraculous signs in the presence of his disciples, which are not recorded in this book. But these are written that you may believe that Jesus is the Christ, the Son of God, and that by believing you may have life in his name" (20:30–31).

7. Seeking miraculous gifts, especially in evangelism, devalues the primacy of the Word of God. The Bible alone is enough to save. Yes, the gospel alone is enough to save, for it is the "power of God for the salvation of everyone who believes" (Rom. 1:16). Tens of thousands have been saved by the Word preached without any attesting works of power. The gospel has intrinsic power to save. The argument of this book, however, is that in the pluralistic world of today, works of power may help the church reach a culture confused by myriad religious choices. In arguing that the postmodern church will be more effective when the Word goes forth with power, is the Word of God devalued?

No, this is exactly what the apostles themselves expressed. They prayed for God to confirm their gospel with works of power. If signs and wonders did not devalue the Word for the apostles, why would they devalue the Word now?

No one has ever preached the Word more powerfully than the apostles. Yet God chose to confirm his words through them with attesting signs and wonders. The argument is frequently made: "The apostles needed that in the first century. Those gifts passed away because the church didn't need them anymore." The suggestion that the church does not need them anymore implies that the apostles needed more help than we do in preaching the gospel! If the apostles, with their tremendous spiritual gifting and ministering to a world that was still filled with eyewitnesses of the resurrected Christ, needed the help of signs and wonders, don't we need them, too?

8. Jesus warns us that in the end times false prophets will work miracles and deceive the elect. Therefore we should not seek miraculous gifts. The work of God's Spirit is always counterfeited by the enemy. The scriptural approach is to learn to discern between true and false prophets. Texts such as Matthew 7:15–17, 2 Peter 2:1–22, and 1 John 4:1–6 guide the church to distinguish the false prophet from the true prophet.

The Bible says there will be false teachers in the end times. Does that mean we should abandon the gift of teaching for fear of being deceived? Jesus did warn his followers to beware of deceiving false prophets who teach error and work false miracles. The fact that Satan can counterfeit a true ministry of the Spirit should not result in rejecting that ministry of the Spirit.

9. The epistles rarely speak of the miraculous gifts. This proves that these gifts passed away toward the end of the first century. The line of this argument says that the gifts are not discussed much in the epistles and that, in the letters written toward the end of Paul's life, we do not find Epaphroditus, Timothy, or Trophimus being supernaturally healed.

This is an argument from silence, which is the weakest kind. Paul does not speak about his gift of celibacy in the later epistles either. Is one therefore to assume that he lost it? Not much can be proved from silence. The epistles do refer to miraculous gifts in Romans 12:3–8, 1 Corinthians 12–14, Galatians 3:5, Ephesians 4:1–16, and 1 Thessalonians 5:20. Moreover, there is no explicit command in the epistles to evangelize. Should one conclude that by the end of the century the apostles had stopped witnessing? Just because Paul did not heal the three men he mentions in the prison epistles does not mean he had lost his gift of healing. The Scripture simply does not say why they were not healed.

The greatest problem with this argument, as Jack Deere points out, is that it contrasts narrative literature with didactic literature. The book of Acts is narrative literature. Luke explained that the purpose of the book of Acts was to tell "about all that Jesus began to do and to teach" (Acts 1:1). Acts is the story of Jesus' continuing his miraculous ministry through the church. The epistles are letters written to churches dealing with specific problems. When the problems related to gifts, as in Corinth, the epistle addressed it. Otherwise there was no reason for the gifts to be mentioned. Furthermore, Paul was in prison when he wrote Ephesians, Philippians, Colossians, and Philemon. These letters will obviously not be filled with stories of Paul working miracles—Paul was locked up![38]

10. The miracles worked by the apostles were always successful, instantaneous, and on the hardest cases (such as organic illnesses like blindness or paralysis). If Jesus and the apostles were here today, they would be emptying the hospi-

tals. The miracles of today are nothing like the ones in the Bible. This proves that the miraculous gifts have ceased.

It has already been affirmed that Jesus and the apostles ministered with extraordinary power. It does not follow from this that believers today cannot minister with these gifts at all. While present-day believers may not witness with that kind of power, they continue to witness. The same is true of these gifts: they may not be used with the power displayed by the apostles, but they are still used.

There does seems to be a distinction between the apostolic gift of healing and the gifts of healing mentioned in 1 Corinthians 12:8–10. These gifts of healing may be of lesser intensity, which would account for the difference between apostolic and modern miracles. Samuel Storms writes:

> [It is repeatedly argued] that the extent and intensity of apostolic signs, wonders and miracles has not continued unchanged throughout church history. I agree. But this would only prove that the apostles operated at a level of supernatural power unknown to other Christians, something virtually everyone concedes. It has no bearing, however, on the question of whether the miraculous gifts of 1 Corinthians 12:7–10 are designed by God for the church in every age.[39]

CONCLUSION

During seminary I had a conversation with my sister-in-law, who had just come to Christ and was involved in a Vineyard church. I told her that the miraculous gifts had ceased. She opened her Bible and asked me to explain why these gifts were no longer for today. God had touched her life with some of these gifts. But she trusted me and sincerely wanted to know why I thought these gifts were not given to the church today.

I stumbled and stalled for about ten minutes. Then, seeing that I wasn't getting anywhere, I said that the key to understanding my point had to do with a particular Greek verb (every seminarian's favorite defense when laypeople trap them.)

That conversation bothered me. The other doctrines I was learning in my seminary classes I could defend clearly and passionately. I couldn't do that with the doctrine of cessation. Years later, I found out why.[40]

IS PAUL REFERRING TO A PERSONAL PRAYER LANGUAGE IN 1 CORINTHIANS 14?

Most New Testament scholars understand Paul to be discussing private prayer language in 1 Corinthians 14. Eugene Peterson expresses this generally accepted interpretation with his version of that chapter in *The Message*. He titles the chapter "Prayer Language." Here is a portion of his translation:

> If you praise him in the private language of tongues, God understands you but no one else does, for you are sharing intimacies just between you and him. . . . the one who prays using a private "prayer language" certainly gets a lot out of it, but proclaiming God's truth to the church in its common language brings the whole church into growth and strength. I want all of you to develop intimacies with God in prayer. But please don't stop with that.

Throughout 1 Corinthians 14, Paul contrasts public tongues speaking in the worship service (which must be interpreted) with another kind of tongues speaking he practices apart from congregational worship. So what kind of tongues speaking is he practicing?

Some have argued that when Paul talks about his own gift of tongues he is referring to his use of tongues for cross-cultural evangelism, as seen in Acts 2. This is unlikely for several reasons. First, nowhere in Scripture is there any evidence that Paul used the gift in this way. Second, the context of 1 Corinthians 12–14 is not cross-cultural evangelism, but worship. Finally, in 14:2, the gift of tongues is described as speaking mysteries to God in the Spirit, which is far more likely to be a description of prayer than of proclamation.

A better understanding of this nonpublic use of tongues is as a private prayer language. Gordon Fee explains:

> Although trying to cool their ardor for congregational tongue speaking, Paul does not disparage the gift itself; rather he seeks to put it in its rightful place. Positively, he says three

things about speaking in tongues. (1) Such a person is "speaking to God," that is, he or she is communing with God by the Spirit.... (2) The content of such utterances is "mysteries" spoken "by the Spirit." ... (3) Such speech by the Spirit is further described in v. 4 as edifying to the speaker.[1]

Paul contrasts public tongues speaking to private tongues speaking in 1 Corinthians 14:18–19: "I thank God that I speak in tongues more than all of you. But in the church I would rather speak five intelligible words to instruct others than ten thousand words in a tongue." Paul prefers using his prayer language privately. A considerable number of commentators understand the passage this way.[2] D. A. Carson comments:

> There is no stronger defense of the private use of tongues, and attempts to avoid this conclusion turn out on inspection to be remarkably flimsy. If Paul speaks in tongues more than all the Corinthians, yet in the church prefers to speak five intelligible words rather than ten thousand words in a tongue ... then where does he speak them? ... *The only possible conclusion is that Paul exercised his remarkable tongues gift in private.*[3]

Such prayer edifies the one praying and allows him to speak mysteries to God (vv. 2–4).[4] Further evidence that Paul is referring to a private prayer language is found in verse 28: "If there is no interpreter, the speaker should keep quiet in the church and speak to himself and God." Here Paul seems to be prescribing the use of tongues when it cannot be interpreted: private prayer to God.

A common misunderstanding of the passage is the view that Paul is condemning private tongues when he says in verse 4, "He who speaks in a tongue edifies himself." This, it is argued, is selfish, since the purpose of spiritual gifts is to edify others. Never, it is argued, is a spiritual gift to be used to edify oneself, nor should a Christian ever seek to edify himself. But Fee echoes the sentiments of many: "Paul intended [to say] no such thing. The edifying of oneself is not self-centeredness, but the personal edifying of the believer that comes through private prayer and praise."[5] Carson retorts that such an argument "scarcely fits the context, when Paul goes on to encourage tongues-speaking (v. 5), which here must be . . . private and for self-edification."[6]

Why would Paul criticize nonpublic tongues speaking as selfish and then tell believers that he wished they all practiced the gift (v. 5), that he personally does it more than they (v. 18), and that the practice should not be forbidden (v. 39)?

Those who desire to pray in a spiritual language have solid biblical justification for doing so.

APPENDIX THREE
FOR LEADERS ONLY

John Maxwell once said that the difference between being a leader and being a martyr is that a leader is one step ahead of his people while a martyr is ten steps ahead. How do we avoid becoming martyrs as we lead our churches through change?

People with leadership gifts see change positively. We have a bias *toward* change. We are constantly reengineering whatever we are a part of to figure out how to do it better. Leaders have been gifted by God with a vision for the future, and we spend our days aligning the present with that future. We see change as a necessary and healthy process. Change motivates us.

People without leadership gifts tend to see change negatively. They have a bias *against* change. Change represents loss, risk, and instability. Every dimension of their world is in transition. The one place where they hope to find security and permanence is the church.

Most people in the church don't have leadership gifts. That is why leaders are so often confused about why people resist change. What we see as wonderful and exciting they see as frightening and dangerous. I am reminded of the 110-year-old man who told an interviewer, "I've seen a whole lot of changes over the past century, and I've been agin' every one of 'em."

We can assume that when we want to bring any type of change into our churches, many people will naturally be against it . . . at first. Encouraging the people to embrace God-brought change is one of the great challenges of spiritual leadership. If you have caught the vision of what God is doing in the world and want to help your church join in, it requires careful, prayerful leadership. Here are some lessons we have learned in trying to embrace the best of both traditions.

Celebrate your heritage. I love my spiritual roots and am very thankful for the rich heritage evangelicalism has given me. Fellowship Church has tried to honor that heritage even as it has embraced some dimensions of the charismatic movement. We have tried to remain who we are while growing into what we can be.

For a number of years some of the literature written by charismatics and evangelicals had the smell of propaganda about it. Many testimonies were the "I was lost but now am found" variety. The body of Christ was divided into good guys and bad guys, the bad guys being whatever group you happened to have just left. This stone-throwing represents our inability to embrace the genius of the AND. Christians have traditionally had a hard time living in tension and saying, "I think there is truth in both places." But this trend is changing.

Never talk negatively about your tradition. Cherish its strengths. Affirm its heroes. Retell its stories. Preach its doctrines. You are not leaving your past as much as you are entering your future.

Begin with your leaders. Never surprise your leaders! They must know what God has put on your heart first and have a chance to talk about it before others in the body do. It is critical to have consensus among the key leaders before you move ahead.

The transition was a painful process for us, as I have already stated. We began discussion with the elders. The next step, after gaining consensus among the staff and elders, was training lay leadership in the vision and values of word and power ministry. We have devoted a number of our leadership training nights to this. I began teaching the theological basis for the merger of word and power. After the doctrinal foundation was in place, we trained leaders in how to shepherd people in a word and power church.[1]

This has been a six-year journey for us, and we are just beginning. I have tried to share with my team along the way what I sense God is saying and doing, taking everything back to Scripture. It is important that the leaders sense together that God is leading the change and that it is not just an idea the pastor obtained from a book or conference.

My hope in writing this book is to speak to the passions of your heart. My prayer is that you will find your heart resonating with my heart, not because of my writing skills, but because of what God is doing in the world today. If this book touches your passions, read it within a leadership team. Talk about the matters you agree with and those you don't. Then begin to pray. What is God doing in your midst? Why did he have one of you read this book? What is he saying? Where is he taking you?

Perhaps one issue emerges as meeting a real need in your church. Begin there.

Find a place to stand doctrinally. As an author addressing the larger body of Christ, I can write, "Whether you call it a baptism of the Holy Spirit or a deeper work, it doesn't really matter. We are all talking about the same thing." As the pastor of a local church, I need to provide doctrinal definition or the flock will become confused. Churches are not seminaries where good people agree to disagree on major doctrinal points. Churches are families and communities where members need to find consensus on core areas.

At Fellowship Church we have had to define what we believe about the authority of Scripture, the prophetic gifts, spiritual language, healing, Spirit baptism, and the role of spiritual gifts in evangelism. Our definitions may well look different from yours. But doctrinal definition is a necessity if a congregation is to maintain unity.

Sometimes our definitions change over time. It is very important that we never operate inconsistently with present doctrinal positions. To do so lacks integrity. Should God change your theology, process this change through the appropriate channels. Pay the price at the doctrinal level, not the practical one.

Remember your mission. Each church has a distinct calling. No church can expect to reach everyone. God raises up different kinds of churches for different kinds of people. Know those whom your church is trying to reach.

The decisions required of you as you embrace the Word and power must be made in light of your unique mission in your community. God is drawing together the two rivers to equip us to reach the lost. What have you learned from this book that will help your church better reach your unique mission field?

At Fellowship we have found the target audience responding to expositional preaching. We also found that they were hungering for participatory worship, so we added this element to our church's philosophy of ministry. We have designed our worship style to be sensitive to the kind of people we attract.

Our target audience is mostly middle- to upper-middle-class professionals. Many of our people carry deep emotional hurts. We saw a need for emotional healing and learned from our charismatic brothers and sisters what a healing ministry looks like. Then we took the principles and worked at applying them to our context. The quiet, relational way we pray for healing fits who we are and whom we are trying to reach.

Whatever you change, *don't* change who you are. Don't tamper with the spiritual DNA that makes your church so special. Whatever you do try to incorporate into your church life, do so in a way that you can say, "This is us."

Keep love the priority. The number-one priority in any change process is preserving loving relationships. Does this mean that we should never make a change that might anger some people and even cause them to leave? No. No leader could make any decision if his only goal was to make sure he didn't upset anyone.

It does mean that it is more important to be loving than to be right. If the congregation is strongly resistant to change in these matters, it is probably unwise to try to lead them through this change. The relational damage that might occur outweighs the benefits on the other side. One pastor I know found his experience and his theology radically changing. He never introduced any of this into his church. Several years later, he left the church on good terms and planted a church consistent with the way he now understood the Scriptures. Today the church numbers four thousand strong and is still growing. I asked this pastor once why he did not try to change his former church. "I have great respect for that tradition and for authority," he said. "I didn't feel I had the right to make those changes in the particular authority structure I was in."

Leadership can be a lonely endeavor. This is especially true when the leader senses the Lord calling him in a new direction. Sometimes God allows us to stay and helps us gently guide our flock through change. Sometimes he calls us to move on and find an environment where we are freed to follow the vision God has put on our hearts.

Another pastor I know who has caught the word and power vision decided to leave a successful, thriving ministry to plant a church where he could follow his passions and convictions more fully. It was a painful, costly choice, but God is blessing him. "I loved where I was," he told me. "But part of me was dying. I had said no to a part of the spiritual life that I knew was true. This was my chance. So I took it."

If you are a layperson, you may want to move forward in these areas and find that your pastor does not share your vision. It is very important at this point to submit to your pastor's leadership. It would be better to leave the church than to work against the pastor's vision.

To paraphrase the apostle Paul in 1 Corinthians 13:1–4: "If you become a word and power church, but do not love your people well along the way, you have failed."

NOTES

Chapter One: My Journey Beyond Categories

1. Jonathan Edwards, *The Religious Affections* (Carlisle, Pa.: Banner of Truth Trust, 1991), 27, 50.

2. Bible scholars point out that the Greek word for spiritual gift is *charisma*, and that in this sense all spiritual gifts are charismatic. However, I'm using the term *charismatic gifts* here in its popular use—that is, referring to the gifts Paul mentions in 1 Corinthians 12:7–10.

3. See the appendix for a summary of the major arguments against cessationism.

4. James C. Collins and Jerry I. Porras, *Built to Last* (New York: HarperCollins, 1997), 44–45.

5. F. Scott Fitzgerald in *The Crack-up* (1936): as quoted in Collins and Porras, *Built to Last*, 45.

Chapter Two: Truce: It's Time to Stop Fighting Yesterday's War

1. Hiroo Onoda, *No Surrender* (New York: Kodansha International, 1974), flyleaf.

2. Onoda, *No Surrender,* 14.

3. *Dictionary of Pentecostal and Charismatic Movements,* ed. Stanley M. Burgess and Gary B. McGee (Grand Rapids: Zondervan, 1988), s.v. "Statistics, Global" by David Barret.

4. Vinson Synan, *The Holiness-Pentecostal Movement in the United States* (Grand Rapids: Eerdmans, 1971), 191.

5. Stephen Strang, "The Holy Spirit Around the World," www.charisma.org.

6. Joseph McAuliffe, "Dominion Work: Reformed Charismatics," *Chalcedon Report* (July 1995).

7. "The Spirit Who Would Not Be Tamed," www.goodnewsmag.org, italics mine.

8. Dennis Rainey, *Pulling Thorns, Planting Seeds* (San Bernardino, Calif.: Here's Life, 1989), 151–52.

Chapter Four: Our Common Heritage

1. Alister McGrath, *Evangelicalism and the Future of Christianity* (Downers Grove, Ill.: InterVarsity Press, 1995), 55-56.

2. Philip Jacob Spener, *Pia Desideria,* trans., ed. Theodore G. Tappert (Philadelphia: Fortress Press, 1964), 87.

3. John Greenfield, *Power on High* (Bethlehem, Pa.: The Moravian Church in America, 1928), 10.

4. J. I. Packer, *A Quest for Godliness* (Wheaton, Ill.: Crossway, 1990), 28.

5. Richard Baxter, *The Reformed Pastor* (Carlisle, Pa.: Banner of Truth Trust, 1989), 147–48.

6. Thomas Goodwin, *An Exposition of the Epistle to the Ephesians*, vol. 1, *Works of Thomas Goodwin* (Edinburgh: James Nichol, 1861), 235–37.

7. Goodwin, *An Exposition of the Epistle to the Ephesians*, 247.

8. Quoted in D. Martyn Lloyd-Jones, *Joy Unspeakable* (Wheaton, Ill.: Harold Shaw, 1984), 150.

9. Lloyd-Jones, *Joy Unspeakable*, 95–96.

10. Charles Wesley in Arnold Dallimore, *George Whitefield*, vol. 1 (Westchester, Ill.: Crossway, 1980), 326.

11. John Cenneck in Dallimore, *George Whitefield*, 327.

12. Quoted in Bernard A. Weisberger, *They Gathered at the River* (Boston: Little, Brown, 1958), 92.

13. Andrew Murray, *In Search of Spiritual Excellence* (Springdale, Pa.: Whitaker House, 1984), 12–14.

Chapter Five: The Legacy of Evangelicals

1. D. Martyn Lloyd-Jones, *Preaching and Preachers* (Grand Rapids: Zondervan, 1972), 26.

2. Oscar Cullman, *Christ and Time* (Philadelphia: Westminster Press, 1964), 37ff.

3. Ken Gire, *Windows of the Soul* (Grand Rapids: Zondervan, 1996), 194.

4. Eugene Peterson, *A Long Obedience in the Same Direction* (Downers Grove, Ill.: InterVarsity Press, 1980).

5. Dallas Willard, *The Spirit of the Disciplines* (San Francisco: Harper-Collins, 1988), 70.

Chapter Six: The Legacy of the Charismatics

1. John L. Sherrill, *They Speak With Other Tongues* (New York: McGraw-Hill, 1964), 83.

2. George Eldon Ladd, *The Gospel of the Kingdom* (Grand Rapids: Eerdmans, 1959), 42.

3. Wayne Grudem, *Systematic Theology* (Grand Rapids: Zondervan, 1994), 1049.

4. Grudem, *Systematic Theology*, 1056.

5. Grudem, *Systematic Theology*, 1070.

6. This summary is found in Barry Leisch, *The New Worship* (Grand Rapids: Baker, 1996), 47–50.

Chapter Seven: In the Presence of a Talking God

1. Bruce Wilkinson, "A Prayer to Ignite Your Life" (Atlanta: Walk Through the Bible Ministries, 1989), cassette tape.

2. John Wimber, *Power Healing* (San Fransisco: Harper & Row, 1986), 44–45.

3. Dallas Willard, *In Search of Guidance* (New York: Harper Collins, 1993), 9–10.

4. Alister McGrath, *Evangelicalism and the Future of Christianity* (Downers Grove, Ill.: InterVarsity Press, 1995), 57.

5. Wayne Grudem, *Systematic Theology* (Grand Rapids: Zondervan, 1994), 73.

6. Ken Gire, *Windows of the Soul* (Grand Rapids: Zondervan, 1996), 216.

7. Eugene Peterson, *Working the Angles* (Grand Rapids: Eerdmans, 1987), 113.

8. Alister McGrath, *Beyond the Quiet Time* (Grand Rapids: Baker, 1995), 10.

Chapter Eight: Not All Speak in Tongues, Do They?

1. Jack Hayford, *The Beauty of Spiritual Language* (Dallas: Word, 1992), 97.

2. Hayford, *Beauty of Spiritual Language*, 19.

3. "Tongues, Updating Some Old Issues," *Eternity* (March 1973): 8.

4. D. Martyn Lloyd-Jones, *The Sovereign Spirit* (Wheaton, Ill.: Harold Shaw, 1985), 48.

5. Sue Schwartz and Joan E. Heller Miller, *The New Language of Toys: Teaching Communication Skills to Children with Special Needs*, 2d ed. (Bethesda, Md.: Woodbine House, 1996), 1.

6. Eugene Peterson, *Working the Angles* (Grand Rapids: Eerdmans, 1987), 111.

7. Walter Ong, *The Presence of the Word* (New Haven, Conn.: Yale University Press, 1967), 309.

8. Jack Deere, *Surprised by the Voice of God* (Grand Rapids: Zondervan, 1996), 358.

9. *Dictionary of Pentecostal and Charismatic Movements* (Grand Rapids: Zondervan, 1988), s.v. "Statistics, Global" by David Barrett.

Chapter Nine: We Need the Caboose

1. Ken Gire, *Windows of the Soul* (Grand Rapids: Zondervan, 1996), 55.

Chapter Ten: Worship Evangelism

1. Diogenes Allen, *Christian Belief in a Postmodern World* (Louisville: John Knox, 1989), 2.

2. Craig Van Gelder, "Postmodernism as an Emerging Worldview," *Calvin Theological Journal* 26 (1991): 413.

3. Walter Truett Anderson, *Reality Isn't What It Used to Be* (San Francisco: Harper & Row, 1990), 75.

4. Leighton Ford, *The Power of Story* (Colorado Springs: Navpress, 1994), 77–78.

5. Douglas Coupland, *Generation X* (New York: St. Martin's Press, 1991), 8.

6. Frederick Dale Bruner, *Matthew* (Dallas: Word, 1987), xiii–xiv.

7. Peter Berger, *The Sacred Canopy* (Garden City, N.Y.: Anchor/Doubleday, 1969), 127.

8. Ramsay MacMullen, *Christianizing the Roman Empire* (New Haven, Conn.: Yale University Press, 1984), 27.

9. Ian Murray, *David Martyn Lloyd-Jones: The First Forty Years* (Edinburgh: Banner of Truth Trust, 1982), 221.

10. Harvey Cox, *Fire From Heaven* (New York: Addison-Wesley, 1995), 86.

11. Rudolf Otter, *The Idea of the Holy*, 2d ed. (London: Oxford University Press, 1950), 12.

Chapter Eleven: Power and Pain

1. Ken Blue, *Authority to Heal* (Downers Grove, Ill.: InterVarsity Press, 1987), 24.

Chapter Twelve: Daily Fillings and Deeper Works

1. Alister McGrath, *Evangelicalism and the Future of Christianity* (Downers Grove, Ill.: InterVarsity Press, 1995), 72.

2. Symeon the New Theologian, *The Discourses in Classics of Western Spirituality*, ed. C. L. deCatauzara (New York: Paulist Press, 1980), 244–46.

3. James Gilchrist Lawson, *Deeper Experiences of Famous Christians* (Anderson, Ind.: Warner Press, 1981), 80.

4. Thomas Goodwin, *An Exposition of the Epistle to the Ephesians*, vol. 1, *Works of Thomas Goodwin* (Edinburg: James Nichol, 1861), 235–37.

5. R. A. Torrey, *The Baptism With the Holy Spirit* (New York: Fleming H. Revell, 1895), 9–14.

6. D. L Moody, "Testimony of D. L. Moody," *Institute Tie* 1 (September 1900): 2.

7. W. R. Moody, *The Life of Dwight L. Moody* (London: Morgan & Scott, 1900), 132–35.

8. D. Martyn Lloyd-Jones, *Joy Unspeakable: Power and Renewal in the Holy Spirit* (Wheaton, Ill: Harold Shaw, 1984), 33–34.

9. M. Scott Peck, *The Road Less Traveled* (New York: Simon & Schuster, 1978), 77.

10. Dallas Willard, *The Spirit of the Disciplines* (San Francisco: Harper Collins, 1988), 156.

11. F. F. Bruce, *The Epistle to the Hebrews* (Grand Rapids: Eerdmans, 1990), 42.

Appendix One: Are Miraculous Gifts for Today?

1. See Wayne Grudem, ed., *Are Miraculous Gifts for Today?* (Grand Rapids: Zondervan, 1996), 10.

2. John Piper, "Compassion, Power and the Kingdom of God: Are Signs and Wonders for Today?" (Sermon preached at Bethlehem Baptist Church in Minneapolis, February 25, 1990).

3. "Tongues, Updating Some Old Issues" (editorial), *Eternity* (March 1973): 8.

4. This view is expressed in John F. MacArthur, Jr., *The Charismatics: A Doctrinal Perspective* (Grand Rapids: Zondervan, 1978), 165–66; Richard Gaffin, *Perspectives on Pentecost* (Philipsburg, N.J: Presbyterian and Reformed, 1979), 109; and Robert Gromacki, *The Modern Tongues Movement* (Philadelphia: Presbyterian and Reformed, 1967), 128–29.

5. Carson calls this the majority interpretation in D. A. Carson, *Showing the Spirit* (Grand Rapids: Baker, 1987), 69.

6. Gen. 32:30; Ex. 33:11; Deut. 5:4; 34:10; Judg. 6:22; Ezek. 20:35

7. D. Martyn Lloyd-Jones, *The Sovereign Spirit: Discerning His Gifts* (Wheaton, Ill.: Harold Shaw, 1985), 33.

8. Some have noted that the verb in verse 8 with "prophecies" and "knowledge" is in the passive voice, and the verb with "tongues" is in the middle voice. They take this to mean that they will cease on their own. Carson replies, "This view assumes without warrant that the switch to this verb is more than a stylistic variation. Worse, it interprets the middle voice irresponsibly. In Hellenistic Greek, the middle voice affects the meaning of the verb in a variety of ways; and not only in the future of some verbs, where middles are more common, but also in other tenses the middle form may be used while the active force is preserved. At such points the verb is deponent. One knows what force the middle voice has only by careful inspection of all occurrences of the verb being studied. In the New Testament, this verb prefers the middle: but that does not mean the subject 'stops' under its own power" (Carson, *Showing the Spirit*, 66–67).

9. For technical treatments of these arguments see Carson, *Showing the Spirit*, 66–72, and Wayne Grudem, *The Gift of Prophecy in the New Testament and Today* (Westchester, Ill.: Crossway, 1988), 227–52.

10. James D. G. Dunn concludes, "The classic Calvinistic view of 1 Corinthians 13:8–13—that glossalia and prophecy [and knowledge] belonged only to the apostolic, or pre-canonical age—is quite foreign to Paul's thought" (James D. G. Dunn, *Jesus and the Spirit* [Philadelphia: Westminster Press, 1975], 424).

11. Lloyd-Jones, *Sovereign Spirit*, 31–33.

12. Benjamin B. Warfield, *Counterfeit Miracles* (1918; reprint, Edinburgh: Banner of Truth Trust, 1972), 235–36.

13. Warfield, *Counterfeit Miracles*, 6.

14. This rationale is the heart of most cessationist arguments since there are no texts to support the position. For a well-reasoned expression of this view, see Richard Gaffin in Grudem, ed., *Are Miraculous Gifts for Today?*, 25–64.

15. Jack Deere, *Surprised by the Power of the Spirit* (Grand Rapids: Zondervan, 1993), 231.

16. Robert Saucy in Grudem, ed., *Are Miraculous Gifts for Today?*, 67.

17. For an interesting study suggesting that Warfield's antisupernaturalist theology was influenced by a branch of Enlightenment thought known as Scottish Common Sense Realism, see Jon Ruthven, *On the Cessation of the Charismata* (Sheffield, UK: Sheffield Academic Press, 1993), 44–52.

18. MacArthur, *Charismatics*, 15.

19. MacArthur, *Charismatics*, 23–26.

20. George Mallone, ed., *Those Controversial Gifts* (Arlington, Tex.: Grace Vineyard of Arlington, 1983), 21.

21. Colin Brown, ed., *The New International Dictionary of New Testament Theology*, vol. 3 (Grand Rapids: Zondervan, 1978), 315.

22. For a survey of signs and wonders in church history, see John Wimber, *Power Evangelism* (San Francisco: Harper & Row, 1986), 156–73.

23. Stanley M. Burgess, *The Spirit and the Church: Antiquity* (Peabody, Mass.: Hendrickson, 1984), 14.

24. *The Didache, Ancient Christian Writers* (New York: Paulist Press, 1948), 21, 22.

25. *Second Apology* vi, *Anti-Nicene Fathers* (New York: Christian Literature Company, 1890–97; reprint, Grand Rapids: Eerdmans, 1953) 1:190.

26. Irenaeus, *Against Heresies*, ii.32.4, *Anti-Nicene Fathers*, 1:409.

27. Origen, *Against Celsus*, I.2, *Anti-Nicene Fathers*, 4:397–98.

28. Hilary of Poitiers, *On the Trinity*, viii.30, *Nicene and Post-Nicene Fathers*, 1st series (New York: Christian Literature Company, 1887–94; reprint, Grand Rapids: Eerdmans, 1952).

29. Augustine, *The City of God*, viii, *Nicene and Post-Nicene Fathers*, 1st series, 2:490–91.

30. S. Baring-Gould, *The Lives of the Saints*, vol. 3 (London: John Nimmo, 1897), 99–100.

31. Howard Watkin-Jones, *The Holy Spirit in the Mediaeval Church* (London: Epworth, 1922), 135.

32. Martin Luther, *Letters of Spiritual Counsel, Library of Christian Classics*, ed. Theodore Tappert, vol. 18 (Philadelphia: Westminster, n.d.), 52.

33. Lloyd-Jones, *Sovereign Spirit*, 46.

34. See Paul Thigpen, "Did the Power of the Spirit Ever Leave the Church?" *Charisma* 18, no. 2 (September 1992): 20–28; Ruthven, "On the Cessation of the Charismata"; Ronald Kydd, *Charismatic Gifts in the Early Church* (Peabody, Mass.: Hendrickson, 1984); Cecil M. Robeck, Jr., "Origen's Treatment of the Charismata in 1 Corinthians 12:8–10" *Charismatic Experiences in History*, ed. Cecil M. Robeck Jr., (Peabody, Mass.: Hendrickson, 1985), 111–25; Donald Bridge, *Signs and Wonders Today* (Leicester, UK: Inter-Varsity Press, 1985), 174ff.; Morton T. Kelsey, *Healing and Christianity* (New York: Harper & Row, 1973), 129–99; James Edwin Davison, "Spiritual Gifts in the Roman Church: 1 Clement, Hermas and Justyn Martyr" (Ph.D. diss., University of Iowa, 1981); and Cecil Robeck, Jr., "The Role and Function of Prophetic Gifts for the Church at Carthage, A.D. 202–258" (Ph.D. diss., Fuller Theological Seminary, 1985).

35. MacArthur, *Charismatics*, 112–14.

36. See Deere, *Surprised by the Power of the Spirit*, 253–66, for a persuasive refutation of this argument.

37. Samuel Storms in Grudem, ed., *Are Miraculous Gifts for Today?*, 187.

38. Deere, *Surprised by the Power of the Spirit*, 238–41.

39. Storms, in Grudem, ed., *Are Miraculous Gifts for Today?*, 159.

40. Wayne Grudem, *Systematic Theology* (Grand Rapids: Zondervan, 1994), 1031–46.

Appendix Two: Is Paul Referring to a Personal Prayer Language in 1 Corinthians 14?

1. Gordon Fee, *The First Epistle to the Corinthians*, NICNT (Grand Rapids: Eerdmans, 1987), 656–57.

2. For example, C. K. Barrett, *First Epistle to the Corinthians* (Edinburgh: T. & T. Clark, 1963), 307: "By communing with God in supernatural language the man who spoke in a tongue built up himself"; Albert Barnes, *1 Corinthians* (Grand Rapids: Baker, 1972), 261: ". . . the truths which are communicated to him by the Spirit, and which he utters in an unknown language, may be valuable and may be the means of strengthening his faith, and building him up in the hopes of the gospel, but they can be of no use to others"; Thomas Edwards, *The Epistle to the Corinthians* (Minneapolis: Klock & Klock, 1979): "He who utters with tongues builds up his own spiritual character, but does not present incentives and encouragements . . . to

his hearers"; F. W. Grosheide, *Commentary on the First Epistle to the Corinthians* (Grand Rapids: Eerdmans, 1953), 318–19: "Glossolalia also has this use that it edifies the one who speaks in a tongue himself . . . speaking in tongues is edifying in itself."

3. D. A. Carson, *Showing the Spirit* (Grand Rapids: Baker, 1987), 105, italics added.

4. Origen and Chyrostom are the earliest scholars to see this gift in Romans 8:26. Modern scholars supporting this view include Hermann Gunkel, Julius Schniewind, Ernst Kasemann, Krister Stendahl, and John A. T. Robinson. (See Frank Macchia, "Sighs Too Deep for Words: Toward a Theology of Glossolalia," *Journal of Pentecostal Theology* 1 [1992]: 59.)

5. Fee, *First Epistle to the Corinthians*, 657.

6. Carson, *Showing the Spirit*, 102.

Appendix Three: For Leaders Only

1. Fellowship Church has put together some of these training materials in a tape series called "The Word and Power Church: Vision and Values." You can order the series by writing to Fellowship Church Tape Ministry, 8000 Middlebrook Pike, Knoxville, TN 37909.

We want to hear from you. Please send your comments about this book to us in care of the address below. Thank you.

ZondervanPublishingHouse
Grand Rapids, Michigan 49530
http://www.zondervan.com